U-Boat 977

U-977 in Argentina

U-Boat 977

The U-Boat that Escaped To Argentina

Preface by
Admiral Of The Fleet
The Earl Of Cork And Orrery, CCB, GCVO.

Foreword by
Nicholas Monsarrat

By Heinz Schaeffer

WRENS PARK

U-Boat 977 was first published in 1952

This edition published in 2003 by Wren's Park Publishing,
an imprint of W. J. Williams and Son Ltd, and by
arrangement with Cerberus Publishing Ltd.

British Library Cataloguing in Publication Data.
A catalogue record for this book is available from the British Library.

ISBN 0 905778 87 1

PRINTED AND BOUND IN GREAT BRITAIN.

Contents

Preface

ADMIRAL OF THE FLEET THE EARL OF CORK AND ORRERY, GCB, GCVO.

Having been asked to express an opinion upon this book I have read it with close attention, and having done so I commend it to all who, whether professionally or otherwise, have their business in great waters.

The story covers the eventful years from 1938 to 1945 in which time the author rose from the rank of cadet to the command of a submarine.

At the close of hostilities, to avoid the surrender ordered, he crossed the Atlantic, making for Argentina, hoping there to find freedom, with the result that he was charged with assisting Hitler to escape to Antarctica,

In this narrative politics are avoided, and no controversy is entered into. The author writes modestly; he tells a straightforward "yarn" which rings true; he is neither aggressive nor apologetic, and what he says can offend no one.

Perhaps the most interesting parts of the story are those which deal with the psychological side – the effect upon men of long and continued strain, of extreme discomfort and boredom, interposed with periods of great danger, and always at the back of their minds the knowledge of the heavy losses being suffered both in men and ships of the submarine service.

It is obvious under these circumstances that the maintenance of a strict discipline is essential. Fundamentally, submarine service in all navies is much the same. In all cases the aim must be to cultivate the military virtues of exact performance of duty, prompt and efficient obedience to orders, alertness and self control, the need of which, whether in peace or war, is apparent to all.

It is due to this continued training, in my opinion, that the list of flag-officers in the Royal Navy contains the names of so many who have served in the submarine branch of that service.

Certainly no one can deny these qualities to the officers of the late German Navy.

If some more undesirable traits seem to have been developed also, it may be due to certain methods of training which the reader can detect for himself.

By the very lucid descriptions given of technical matters touched upon, the story is made as interesting for the uninitiated as it is for those who have some knowledge of the subject. These details allow the ebb and flow of the submarine battle to be followed, the sway of advantage from one side to the other as new instruments and devices appear, and before counter measures have been perfected; e.g. a chapter devoted to Radar is headed "The Worst Enemy" and the reason for this is made very clear.

No one need avoid the book on the grounds that it would be "too technical".

There are also interesting sidelights recounting the author's reflections when he visited his relatives on his rare periods of leave from the height of success to the lowest depths of defeat.

The description of the voyage to the Argentine is an epic in itself – sixty days under water!

This is a good story well told, and reveals the author as an efficient and brave officer and a man of determined character.

Foreword

NICHOLAS MONSARRAT

There is a current Anglo-American illusion, skillfully fostered during the war, that whereas the Germans used U-boats, which were beastly, we only used submarines, which were quite different, and rather wonderful. (This piece of self-delusion does not persist with those who have ever been at the receiving end of a torpedo.) Of course, there is another side to the medal. It cannot be denied that submariners of any nation are brave and skillful men: and that they are accustomed to continue to exercise their skill in conditions of acute danger, which is perhaps the bravest thing of all. But what they actually do, what constitutes their life working by stealth, without warning and without quarter – is evil as well as skillful; moreover, it is predominantly evil, and, when we come to our senses, inexcusably so.

Here then is U-boat 977, a book by a brave and skillful man who was the instrument of this evil tradition. In writing a foreword to such a book, I am not acting on any forgive-and-forget principle; the author, and men like him, were trying to kill me and my friends for five years on end in the Battle of the Atlantic, and I loathed and feared them for it, and I loathe them still. But it is right that, when the fight is over and the U-boats defeated, we should try to learn something of the other side of the picture: that we should know what it was like at the opposite end of the periscope, that we should understand what made these men tick – and, in ticking, kill.

We do learn all these things from this book, and that is why it should be read. We learn of the training of young U-boat men, and of their initiation in this special kind of murder. We learn what they felt like when they got their quarry in their sights – and, alternatively, their feelings when, as often happened, they became the quarry themselves, and the depth-charges started to crack and thunder about their ears. The author was, for much of the war, a U-boat commander, and, I should say, a good one, or he would not be alive today; we learn what that was like, too, and the tremendous strain of such a command.

We learn of the coming of Radar to the war at sea, that vital weapon that changed the whole complexion of the fight and, at long last, evened the scale between U-boat and escort. We learn, by inference, of the tremendous cost of maintaining the Allied life-line across the Atlantic, with the U-boat packs sometimes falling upon a convoy and ripping it to ribbons, sometimes being bloodily beaten off in the act of attack. We understand, in fact, what we only guessed at and feared in those bad vanished days.

The book closes with the escape of U-977 to the Argentine, at the end of the war. This is in itself a remarkable story; the voyage took three-and-a-half months, with the crew sometimes disciplined, sometimes on the edge of mutiny; and at one time the U-boat spent sixty-six consecutive days under water - a feat of endurance and determination which deserves every tribute But there is always something else, in a story like this; and for me, the high-light of this book is a small incident in the early part of it, which describes the sinking of a tanker.

She was sunk in the North Atlantic, breaking in two in wild weather. There was, of course, no warning given; simply the sighting, the stalking, the hand on the trigger, the sweet moment of murder. When it was all over, the author tells us, when the survivors had been left to die, and the wrecked ship extinguished by the sea, "we put on some gramophone records, and hear the old songs that remind us of home".

The book includes also, to make us burst into tears, a sigh for something which other U-boats, failing to reach the Argentine, apparently looked for in vain: a "decent respect for the defeated".

Ah, Germany!

But read it for yourselves. It is valuable, as I said, for its authentic picture, close to and sharply focused, of this kind of warfare. It is more valuable still for the inferential story, the crude driving-force behind it all, the reason for which U-boats came into being in the first place. Reading it, absorbing its filthy and violent outlines, we know just how far politics can travel on the road to insanity, and what men can do to other men in their greedy lust for power.

Preface to the First Edition

After the First World War men who had seen active service were quick to express themselves in print because under the circumstances of the time they felt able to tell their story in full. But few Germans who survived the Second have broken their silence yet, and the reason apparently is that their ordeal seems to have been futile and their future, in a swiftly changing world over-shadowed by the threat of yet another war, uncertain to say the least. I am only one of those unknown young Germans who came through the Second World War, and I too would keep silent if I only could. But the mystery of U-977 has already been the subject of so much comment that I feel impelled to tell my story. For I was its last Commander, and as I am now living abroad I can speak more freely than those who are back at home. I was conscious of the weight of my responsibility as soon as I began to write my book, for, apart from the despatches of Günther Prien, who lost his life in the early days of the fighting, I know of no other U-boat Commander in the war of 1939-45 who has set pen to paper.[1] Those most qualified to speak are either at the bottom of the sea or else have been so caught up in the struggle for survival in the post-war world that they have not been able to find the time to write. I am only one of many unknown German sailors, and I write with no more authority than any other who simply carried out his orders. I am afraid that means very little in comparison with what might be claimed by others far more distinguished than myself. But it does mean something when you reflect that while there have been one or two good books written from the German side about the fighting on land and in the air, nobody has yet told the story of what we did at sea in this most terrible of all international struggles.

[1] Since the first publication of this book a number of U-Boat commanders have written their stories – some are included in the 'Fortunes of War' series.

Yet, while both on land and in the air Germany started off as strong as her enemies and backed by a powerful industrial machine, at sea we were always up against superior odds and had to make up for our scanty material resources by our own efforts and skill. Although I feel we can claim to have done this, those efforts nevertheless made enormous demands on the individual. The way that German sailors stood up to those demands is not the least of the chapters in the history of this war.

From a personal point of view my own experience was in some ways unique, as I was Commander of a submarine that accomplished one of the first long distance voyages underwater in human history, and led me into complications of a political kind at the highest level, which are described in the last chapter of this book.

It is this above all that has induced me to tell my story.

I dedicate my work to my ship's company who stood by me all through that memorable voyage to the Argentine, to my mother who roused my interest in the sea while I was still a child, and to my wife who so tirelessly helped me in writing this tribute to the men of the German submarine forces.

HEINZ SCHAEFFER
Buenos Aires
September 1950

CHAPTER ONE

YESTERDAY

POST-WAR fate transplanted me, Berliner though I am, to Düsseldorf on the Rhine. That once lovely, lively town was barely recognisable. I went for a stroll through the city centre, and found all around me shabby, haggard people, the skeletons of what had been houses, and the foreign uniforms of the Occupation troops. Wandering meditatively along the Königstrasse, I happened to pass a newspaper stall: a down-at-heels newsvendor was screeching at the top of his voice, "Hitler alive!"

I looked more closely at the headline. And underneath I saw in smaller type, "Fled to the Argentine aboard U-977".

I was one of very few who bothered to buy a copy. I made for a café with it under my arm, and over a glass of watery post-war beer I assessed this latest "bombshell". It was an agency report from Buenos Aires about a book by a certain Ladislas Szabo just published in the Argentine capital. It claimed that U-530, my brother-officer Wehrmut's ship, and U-977, my own – the only two units of the former German Navy still at large, and which had appeared off the Argentine coast long after the capitulation – formed part of a ghost convoy which had carried Hitler and other "big shots" of the Third Reich first to the Argentine, and then to the Antarctic. the paper even gave the itinerary followed by the "phantom Convoy", including the point at which the two submarines had separated from it. It also stated that the two Commanders concerned were ready to vouch for the truth of the story.

However laughable might be some of its aspects, this account also had its more disagreeable associations as far as I was concerned, for since the 17th August 1945 the accusation had been constantly levelled at me: ,'You, Schaeffer, are the man who took Hitler to the Argentine!" Whether I had to do with the special Allied Commission which had landed at Buenos Aires or with the American intelligence officers who sent me off by air to Washington to undergo interrogation by British Admiralty experts, I had to fight for all I was worth to exculpate myself.

The importance which was attached to my case at Washington is not easy to forget. I was regarded as one of the main clues necessary for the solution of more than one political Mystery. "It's because you helped Hitler to escape, Schaeffer," I was told, "that you are considerably more interesting from our point of view even than Skorzeny, who set Mussolini free."

By this time it was getting dark. I trekked back to my dreary bachelor lodging and tried to get some sleep. But the news report from Buenos Aires had stirred a flood of memories.

Over in the drawer of my desk lay the crumpled notebooks that told in full the true story of the "mysterious" voyage of U-977 and of myself, Heinz Schaeffer, the man who "stowed Hitler away". Those books recorded accurately every phase of my career at sea. As I turned the pages they still gave out that characteristic, comforting aroma of oil, pitch and sea-water which impregnates everything on board a submarine. My own writing was a faithful enough reflection of my state of mind from day to day. Sometimes, as with the careful calligraphy of my time at training-school, it was calm and level, at others a mere "telegraphic" pencil scrawl when I was in contact with the enemy. Finally there were sixty-six pages so clearly legible that they might have been written by a schoolboy.

Now I could see myself on 17th August 1946, back at anchor in the port of Mar del Plata surrounded by Argentine warships. The Flotilla Commander comes aboard with his staff. My crew are fallen in on deck. I deliver my report in German. The Argentinian doesn't understand a word, yet clearly he grasps the importance of this occasion. Can I speak French? Now at last we have a common medium.

Within half an hour at the latest we must all be out of the boat. The men can keep their gear and I may make a farewell speech to my crew.

Somehow I managed to strike the right note to express the depth of our feelings. My throat was dry, and I had to cough to clear it.

"*Kamoraden*," I began, "as we set out to do on the 9th of May of this fateful year, we have put into an Argentine port. I am sure we have done right. None of us will ever regret this voyage. For most of us it will always remain the greatest experience of our lives, an achievement of which we can be proud. This is a hard parting for us after all we have been through together. Our very existences have been so closely interlocked that we have become almost a single being, but now each individual will be master of his fate and free to go his own way. But we must never forget that we are German sailors, survivors of the most formidable arm of this whole war. That thought will be a bond between us in the years to come. I thank you for your trust and loyalty. I wish you each fulfilment of his hopes and the attainment of his desire."

After that I shook hands with them all for the last time. There was emotion in every bearded weatherbeaten face, and tears glistened in many eyes. But I had to keep a hold on myself and play the man of iron to the end. Last of all I gave my hand to our Moses, the youngest hand on board,

"I'm not worrying about you, my lad," I said, "you'll land on your feet all right. Good luck to you, Moses."

And so we had to bid our faithful boat goodbye. Across the sun-flecked waters of Mar del Plata a German order rang out for the last time.

" *Besatzung stillgestanden!* Three cheers for our loyal, our invincible U-977. Hip, hip, hurrah!"

The Argentine officers watched the little farewell ceremony with the respect of fighting men. Then they ordered me and my officers on board the flagship. I had kept all my log-books, charts and navigational data, and I took these with me.

On the deck of the cruiser *Belgrano* Argentine submarine crews were fallen-in. The band was playing a march as we climbed up the gangway. I reported with my officers to the duty officer and together with us he walked along the ranks of sailors in white uniforms. And though I didn't yet know how German soldiers and sailors were being treated in other countries and other ports – like whipped dogs without respect or regard – I was grateful for this chivalrous gesture to the vanquished.

In the wardroom I was asked to make a full report about our passage as indicated by the charts. Then I had to explain to the Submarine Flotilla Commander why I hadn't sunk any boat offshore. I told him that had we done so we could never have brought the true facts of our voyage to light.

But how little it mattered what we said was apparent from his reply.

"Captain, I must tell you that your boat is suspected of having sunk the Brazilian steamship *Bahia* a few days ago. It is also suspected that you had Adolf Hitler, Eva Braun and Martin Bormann on board and put them ashore somewhere on the southern part of our continent. Both these matters must be cleared up immediately."

Confidently I spread my charts out on the table and traced out our course since 9th May.

"If these charts are correct," he conceded, "at the time of her sinking you were 60 miles from the spot where the *Bahia* was sunk. However, we shall check your papers."

The officers clearly had no intention of dragging on the interrogation that day before they had inspected my ships papers and an interpreter had arrived from Buenos Aires. Next we were officially informed that we were prisoners of war. I was separated from my brother officers and conducted to a spacious officer's cabin, where I found a bottle of good Scotch whisky on the table.

Two sentries were posted outside. After many, many months I was alone for the first time, alone with my memories and my responsibilities.

How was it that my war had ended almost a hundred days after the capitulation of the Wehrmacht? How was it that, with my boat intact and all my documents, I had entered a harbour which had ranked as an enemy one since March of this same year? How had they been led to believe that Hitler was on board her?

CHAPTER TWO

White Sails to Grey Wolves

BERLIN, my native city, is my earliest memory – Berlin, with its long prospects of busy, crowded streets, its houses and its hard-working, good-natured people, the city which has left its mark on all Germany.

But for me Berlin stands mostly for the shimmering belt around it: the waters of its rivers and canals, the gleaming stretches of its lakes luring you on into the distance and the still and silent inlets beckoning you to linger. I can still see the lofty pine trees of Brandenburg mirrored in those waters, and myself as a boy of five.

"When I grow up I'm going to be a sea-captain," I told my mother as she stood over my bed, begging me to take more care not to fall into the water again. But that was nothing new by now. I could already swim as well as any little water-rat.

Although I was soon an expert oarsman my attention was presently diverted by the sight of sailing ships speeding along the waterways, and I looked on enviously while my friends glided by apparently without effort under the spread of their sails. Before long some of my friends and I hit upon the idea of converting my father's fishing-boat – though in fact I never knew anyone to fish from it – into a craft of a rather different nature. It was the perfect time for us to set about the job as Father was away shooting and Mother busy stewing fruit for bottling. So my friends and I went ahead and soon got things moving, fitting up a bean stick as a mast and hammering washing-lines onto it with iron nails for rigging.

Our first effort in sail was encouraging. With a following wind we managed to sail several hours upstream. But when we were beating against the wind things were rather different, You can't tack without an adequate keel, and lee-boards are the best alternative. We had often seen passing barges make to windward with lee-boards, and so we set to work to make some. There was plenty of wood in our garden; we managed to lay hands on a supply of nails; and after we had secured our makeshift boards the sides of the boat looked rather like the kind of bed fakirs lie down on. Naturally, water came seeping in everywhere. Boys are often first-rate improvisers but they have a habit of smashing things without meaning to. At the first squall we went spinning round, and our fine sailing-ship was swamped, mast and all, in a twinkling.

"If you carry on like that it won't be the last ship you'll sink," said my father, as he confined me to the house under a sort of arrest. I wonder if he guessed how exactly his prediction would come true.

The years passed by, and, with my childhood behind me, I joined the junior branch of a famous yacht club. One never-to-be-forgotten Sunday in spring 1934, I came upon this statement on the club notice board: "Will junior member Heinz Schaeffer report to the club committee." So with my heart beating I stood before the president, who sat at a massive table covered with a grey cloth. He was a well-known figure in the commercial world, with a whole array of handles to his name.

"How would you like to be the boatswain of the schooner *Sonnenwender*?" he asked me. My eyes lit up at the undoubted compliment of being chosen by the owner of such a fine sailing-ship. Naturally I knew there was a great deal of work attached to the job, but I had much to learn before I could pass my tests in sail and so qualify to take over a club boat at a regatta.

"*Jawohl*" I replied at once, and so bound myself over for the season, and duly signed my name on the club register, which was modelled on the roll of the Merchant Service. I knew very well that if I proved unfit for my duties I would be struck off, but I was determined never to incur such a terrible disgrace as that.

From that day on I was always ready at seven o'clock on Saturdays to carry out my honorary duties as boatswain to my lord and master. Only thirteen, and the youngest hand working on any of our ships, I would make everything shipshape and dress myself up in spotless white to welcome my employer. When he did come, with his family and friends, as there was only room for three people in the dinghy besides myself and as the yacht lay at anchor about a hundred yards from the landing-stage, I had to make four journeys and was pretty well exhausted by the time I finished the last.

"We don't want to waste any time, Heinz; we should be off in half an hour."

So I would begin making ready, while they all sat enjoying themselves and drinking beer. When it came to hoisting the sails, as luck would have it a halyard went to the masthead, and then of course I had to go aloft. It was a 60-foot climb and the very thought of it made me giddy, but I dared not show how frightened I was, and up I went.

So with a strong wind blowing we glided down stream. I would have clearly loved to steer that 16-ton two masted schooner. But my job was to keep her clean. I also had to clean out the bilges and careen her, so I soon began to look very dirty. It wasn't exactly my idea of fun, but there was no help for it I just had to keep quiet and get on with the job. "Experience is all that counts", my Captain would say, so I had to do every job there was to do. I even had to wash up, which I had never done at home, and a nice mess I made of it. On top of everything else, the second time we went sailing we were becalmed on the way home. I got going like a galley-slave and tried to make headway towing the boat with the dinghy. But it was just too bad if the owner found me slacking, for he'd soon pull me up sharp enough. I could only hope that I was doing my job well enough not to be thrown out.

Sometimes I felt I might as well build a new boat, since I had to renew all the rigging, oil the various pulleys and make new splices. Every day there was something to be polished up and varnished, for my skipper was a retired naval officer and thorough to a degree. He always made a fine showing when there was a race. Later on I was allowed to handle the jib myself, and in the end I actually did steer the boat. It was a proud day for me when I told my father I had passed all the tests and was now qualified to take charge of any sailing-boat on the rivers and inland waterways of Germany. By all the rules I was too young at fourteen to hold a certificate of that kind, but my skipper managed to get it through for me.

From now on I was my own master. Father gave me a racing dinghy which was about 23 feet long and 4 feet across, a perfect boat to sail in a regatta. I spent every spare moment I could find aboard her, picking up all kinds of tips from the club experts. For every strength of wind you need stiffeners of different thickness, and you must set your mast correctly for each change of trim. Every inch – every fraction of an inch even – can be vital. The smoothness, too of the hull below the waterline is very important. Everyone had his own recipe and I had mine, which was first to go over the keel with graphite on a cork and then wax it thoroughly and polish it up till it shone like a looking-glass, and then finally add the finishing touch, a compound of eggs and oil.

At last the day of my first race arrived. As soon as the starting-gun went off, though there was a strong following wind, we put on all sail so as to make the best use of the calm waters inshore. We soon shipped a good deal of water. Hans, at the jib, worked wonders baling out with one hand, trimming the jib with his other, and leaning over the side at the same time to keep the balance even. The worst stretches came when we felt the full force of the following wind – three competitors had already fallen out. Usually in calm waters you hoist a spinnaker for'ard which trebles the drawing-power of a sailing-boat. We hadn't hoisted one yet, but we were left far behind so up it went and we risked it.

We shot through the water like an arrow, carrying three times the spread of canvas for which our boat was designed. Soon we drew level with the leading boats. Things were not going particularly well, for we found it hard to keep on our course. But others were doing worse – their efforts to follow our example were disastrous. Two capsized and three ripped their precious balloon-silk sails into shreds and gave up. We kept well ahead, and after six hours of it were awarded the third prize.

I took part in several more regattas, in which sometimes I was lucky, sometimes not. But I was nearly always up against well-known yachtsmen who boasted titles like "All German Champion" and "Olympic winner" and who had a new boat built every year, which made competition very difficult. All in all, the whole time I was at school my heart was in sail, so it was hardly surprising that my reports were consistently bad, Still, I did manage to keep all my terms, though I went to six different schools, sometimes changing of my own free will and sometimes not.

I was best at mathematics; other subjects seemed to me to demand too much cramming, and I never could manage to memorise things.

In 1938 my father sent me out to the United States. The sea voyage itself was a delightful experience for me and I certainly got a great deal of interest and instruction from the trip. While I was out there I went to high school at Cleveland, and of course it all helped to improve my English.

When I got home the question of my career was broached. For a long time my family had set their minds on forestry, as I always had been interested in nature studies, woodcraft and shooting. But the lure of water, so obviously my element, was stronger still.

I was young, and the idea of being a naval officer with all that it implied was highly attractive to me. Besides, at the sailing-club we often used to meet naval officers, and I was very impressed with them, for they were so obviously practical, experienced people with a knowledge of the world, used to wind and weather and technical matters in general,

As for the idea of war, it scarcely occurred to me. That things could ever come to such a pass I never seriously imagined. Boys simply don't think that way. Of course if it did come there was only one thing to do, namely one's duty, in whatever station one happened to be.

I never had the slightest interest in politics. The circles in which I moved had no contacts with the world of Nazism or the Nazi creed, and I never joined the Hitler Youth Movement. True, in my last year at school I did some voluntary work on the land during the summer holidays, which I thoroughly enjoyed. In fact, the chairman of the local parish council thanked me officially, which duly impressed the school authorities. But I took good care to keep out of any organisation, except of course the sailing club.

Naturally I realised that as an officer I would have to obey all orders without question. But I knew too that it would be in a service where every man has his own duties and responsibilities, a service bound by its own traditions and the code it has built up.

I persuaded my father to let me take the examinations for a naval cadetship during my last year at school – I had already sent in a hand-written account of my career hitherto, together with the other necessary documents. The exams, which were to last fourteen days, fell towards the end of the Christmas term 1938.

When I arrived at Kiel things quickly started moving. Innumerable psychologists were always observing us. At our medicals the oddest things were done to us. We had to sit in an enormous chest, while on a great board we saw lights go on at regular intervals which we had to extinguish with special levers. Whenever they went out by themselves we lost a mark. There were also two sirens and a bell under our seat which we had to work simultaneously with our feet. This was a test during which many of us lost our heads completely.

Our special terror was an electric-shock machine, our reactions to which the authorities were most keen to observe. We had often heard that white of egg is a good insulator and this we rubbed all over our hands, but I must admit that both in my own and my friends' case it didn't work at all, and we just had to stand up to the ordeal as best we could. We had to grasp the two ends of a bar, and once the apparatus was switched on and the current began to flow we couldn't let go of them. Many of us just screamed – quite the wrong thing – but others bit their cheeks and by drawing them in gave an impression of stern endurance. All this was filmed, but we never saw the film, though it must have been an interesting one.

When it came round to testing our languages I naturally got high marks in English.

Our superiors also wanted to see if we knew how to behave at table, and as the exam lasted fourteen days they had every chance to find that out. We were duly presented to several high-ranking officers. Such occasions were apt to be stuffy as etiquette was never relaxed, and things were no easier when it came to making conversation with their wives and daughters, who were liable to be very touchy about their dignity. Luckily we were always introduced by someone else and didn't have to present ourselves, for I doubt whether any of us would have been up to that. At last we would all resort to a long table among officers with endless rings on their sleeves, where we all sat very stiff and upright, fearful of what was coming next. We glanced carefully right and left, for we might so easily go wrong, and it would probably be well to follow the officers' example. But that didn't help us much because every officer behaved differently, on purpose of course, none having the slightest intention of helping us out. In any case some of them sat with their arms and legs hunched up, while others poured their own wine out without calling a steward; in fact their manners were in general quite impossible, and it turned out to be just too bad if anybody fell into the trap by trying to imitate them.

The table was laid with glasses and plates and apparently all the rest of a normal table service, but with the odd knife, fork, or spoon missing. Of course we could start eating something we liked and wait till we needed the missing implement, but no one ever got very far like that, and a friend of mine who skillfully abstracted a spoon from an elderly Captain was soon spotted by the watching psychologists. Others did the right thing straight off and asked the stewards to bring them the cutlery they needed. The whole affair was a lively mix-up all round.

Dessert was the high spot, consisting of little yellow plums or mirabelles, which looked extremely appetising. But we didn't see the trap ahead. The only things left on the table were teaspoons, but it's quite impossible to cut up a mirabelle with a teaspoon and equally impossible to put one into one's mouth whole. If someone did venture on this last course he was certain to be asked a question or have his health drunk, and then he would go red in the face and look very silly indeed. I was particularly unlucky because when I tried to cut up mine with my teaspoon it shot off and landed plumb on my adjacent psychologist's butterfly collar. I apologised, asked the steward to bring some water to erase the stain, and went on to eat what was left with my fingers, as by then I was getting a bit fed up.

When the exams ended at last, I was allowed to go home, where in due course I learnt that I had passed. As my visit to the United States, however much it broadened my outlook, could not make up for all the deficiencies in book learning I had to make good before I passed my finals at Easter, I decided to put off the second trip I had in mind until the autumn.

But by then war had broken out. We were embarked on a tremendous struggle, although when it started no one realised its full implications or dreamt of the eventual outcome. The campaign in Poland ended very quickly, but no one knew what was going to happen after that. I naturally wondered what lay in store for me. Here was I about to go in the Navy, which was obviously destined to play a vital role in the war against Britain, the greatest seapower in the world. But luckily I had no time to dwell on problems of naval strategy for I still had all my training to do.

Late in 1939 I travelled to the training-school at Stralsund. In the train that took us northward from the Stettiner Bahnhof we were easily recognisable by our close-cropped hair – we knew how important it was for recruits to have their hair cut. At Stralsund Station some petty officers were waiting to marshal us into formation, and so, singing gaily, we swung along towards Dänholm, an island used exclusively for training purposes. It was bitter winter weather, fourteen below zero, but in spite of the cold we soon got warm at the brisk pace we had to keep up. A swing-bridge which lifted as soon as we had crossed was eloquent of our temporary segregation from the outside world.

After we had passed the two guardrooms we found ourselves in the naval barracks area. The sentries all grinned as we went by, for they knew that our high spirits would soon be dampened once the petty officers got going on us, and on Dänholm they did it the rough way. They were all failed officer trainees themselves and now they had the chance to go through the whole course from start to finish again, from a rather more detached standpoint, assuming they didn't decide to retire from the service voluntarily. The only catch was that when trainees did retire their fathers forfeited the eight hundred marks caution money that every trainee had to put down in case he failed to reach the required standard.

We had to spend three months on Dänholm, and I can't pretend I liked it. I cannot, now that I come to look back on them in detail, really justify all the things that went on there. But of course there is another side to it all. One must beware of going to the other extreme and brooding tragically over the time when one got knocked around a bit. Even if armies do exist whose members would flinch at the sort of treatment we took in our stride, the Prussian NCO is, I am sure, not by any means a unique phenomenon. As long as there are establishments run on military lines in the world the recruit will be treated rough and licked painfully into shape.

Eight men on the average shared a "cabin", and sixteen of us again formed a section. There were four sections to a platoon and four or five platoons to a company. We turned out at six, but we weren't just piped out of our bunks at the first stroke of the hour, before rushing to the wash-house. Instead, we were treated to a long prelude on a whistle which I found a positive martyrdom. Every order in the German Navy was preceded by a sort of overture on the boatswain's whistle – he could not only blow it in different keys, but also add his own variations by trilling his tongue. So before we were actually turned out he would gradually work up a crescendo, beginning softly and gradually bringing his piping to a climax. I found this the most nerve-racking part of my whole training. By degrees you get so used to the whistle that you can detect it a long way off, and as it's always blowing somewhere you hardly get a moment's peace the whole day long. When we were out of our bunks, after the second blast on the whistle and the call *Reise, Reise*, or some such nautical ballad had been piped, we all went off to the wash-house at the double, took our turns under the shower and shaved. Cadets detailed to act as stewards had to jump to it, as they had to bring up our breakfast and then clear the tables, operating from a galley a quarter of a mile away.

Early days were on the whole, however, comparatively peaceful. We were issued with one grey uniform, two white ones and two blue ones with overalls, along with a rifle and a gas-mask, with which we were supposed to be particularly pleased. After we were sworn in things started moving.

We learnt how to carry ourselves and stand upright. It was forever draw in your stomach, throw out your chest, keep your fingers back; salute sitting, standing, running. After two hours' drill we had an hour's lecture. But then we only had to sit straight and look attentive.

The actual learning presented no differculties – we all had eleven to twelve years of school behind us and had our *Abiturientenzeugnis*, or school-leaving certificate. The purpose of the first three months was not to teach us much but rather to take note of our character and our behaviour, weed out the ones who reacted against the harsh discipline and throw them out. Our training was based on the theory that only those who know how to obey are fit to command.

At six in the evening we were free and had a meal, the officers scattered among us so that they could make informal contact with us. Then we had two hours to ourselves. Finally, after a thorough "clear up decks", "stand by hammocks" was piped and we turned in. Fifteen minutes after came the order "Lights out. Silence." But that didn't mean we were left in peace from ten to six. "Rounds", as performed by the boatswain's mate, could easily make things hot for us.

On these occasions everybody in the mess would stand in front of his open locker and wait for the inspecting officers, the mess captain, who was responsible for every minute detail, shouting "*Achtung!*" – the louder the better.

"Mess Captain Müller reports mess five with eight men mustered for mess and locker inspection."

"Good evening, mess five."

"Good evening, boatswain's mate, sir."

"Asleep already? On top of your lockers! Jump to it! Your fingers, Schulze! Off to a funeral, are you? Why then the mourning bands? Knees bend ten times can't you count louder? Take ten more. Meier, do you call that locker tidy? Knees bend twenty times. What's that woman's picture doing in your locker? Yes, it's you I'm speaking to. What's it there for? You ought to have some Admiral's picture to set you an example." Two people grinned. "What's so funny about it? Out onto the parade ground and make it snappy!"

He would come out behind us, and for a quarter of an hour there would be hell. At the end of this morale-boosting we had to parade with kitbags packed – everybody had a great bag into which he had to stow his gear. It wasn't so hard to pack, as to get everything back in the locker shipshape.

Our seniors had plenty to tell us about the Valley of Death. It was part of every course, the peak of the ordeal we had to undergo. We knew quite well that any silly excuse would do as a pretext for acquainting us with that delightful spot, and one day it happened. The boatswain's mate had ordered my squad to fall in on the parade ground for a route march. The squad commander received his orders and we went ahead, a pack weighing 52 pounds on our backs, arms sloped, and a gas-mask slung at our waists.

Change – arms! At the double! Right and left we dashed according to the word of command and in step with those in charge, who always took the shortest cross country cuts. We were off to the Valley of Death. We had to cross two hills with a valley between them, and there the men fell out who couldn't make the second hill. But you couldn't just fall out and so escape the strain, for anyone who didn't come through was not up to the physical standard required of an officer and was thrown out of the training-school. The best thing was to make provision by having a shore-job ready just in case. Everyone put all he had into it to avoid being branded as a slacker. We used to hear of people contemplating suicide – it was so disgraceful to be chucked out that they thought they would never dare to face the world again. That spirit among the officer corps was not the least of the factors that enabled our leaders to carry on the war so long.

Once down in the Valley of Death the order would be snapped out, "Up now on the other side, jump to it!"and so on for an hour, all the time with rifles in your hands and heavy packs on our backs. Many would fall out for a moment, but then pull themselves together and go on, uphill, downhill, uphill again most of us went scarlet in the face, and some went blue. But we were all thinking, "I can't go on; any more of this will just kill me."

But there was plenty more to come. Once again we were back at the foot of the first hill, scarcely able to stand on our feet. "Gas!" It was the command to don our gas-masks. Breathless as we were, this was the worst thing conceivable. Like a knife cutting the deep silence rang out the sharp voice of our squad leader: "Don't you *want* to do any more, or *can't* you?" One of us had to drop out. Next time another. My companions lagged along behind each other. But at last came the word of command that brought our release. "Fall in on the road – *sing!*"

So we went back to barracks. Luckily we had nothing but lectures for the next few hours.

There was also exercise Dead Man, which, unlike the Valley of Death, only, involved one hill.

Then we had exercise Arctic Dress. We had to put on all the clothing we had, and an amazing amount it was: three sets of pajamas, sports gear, two blue uniforms, grey overcoat, woollen cap, gloves, steel helmet, knapsack and much more besides. A room was cleared and the heating apparatus turned full on. Our squad could just about cram inside. Twenty press-ups! That meant, lie on your stomach, arms stretch and arms bend. Then knees bend, take up your rifles. It went on till we were boiling all over. Everybody was itching. We thought we should collapse. Our only consolation was that nothing lasts for ever.

Actually those three months' intensive training passed quite quickly. We practised throwing hand-grenades, machine-gunning and rifle-shooting, in which I did pretty well, as I had had many chances to show my marksmanship on our own estate and out shooting with my father. My awards for marksmanship delighted him, as he had won them himself when he was in the Army. The purpose of our first three months was to teach us the essentials of a soldier's life and had very little to do with naval training.

One thing that reminded us that we were sailors, for such we called ourselves, was the fact that we had a blue walking-out uniform. Everybody knew that we were officer cadets. Our cap-bands displayed the golden letters 7.S.St.A. – *Siebente Schiffstammabteilung* (7th Naval Training Unit) – and that was a red rag to all NCOs in the Army and the Luftwaffe stationed at Stralsund. It was their last chance to take it out of us, for in a year we would probably all be midshipmen and free from donkey-work. So everybody went for us with genuine delight and drafted complaints to the training-school about slackness in saluting and such-like trivialities, for which we received due punishment. We weren't left in peace a minute once we ventured outside the area of naval barracks.

Our last exercise and passing-out parade was on the grand scale. We were issued with blank cartridges, smoke-bombs and other battle equipment, and stormed trenches and forts, always showing our zeal by making a great deal of noise.

After this I had to appear before my section officer. "The reports on you have been extremely bad," he told me. "We've been discussing at great length whether you should not remain here, but you're a good shot and in these times that is, after all, the main thing. So we're going to transfer you to a training unit on probation, where I hope you'll do better."

"*Jawoh!*" and I hurried joyfully out of the room. I had crossed my first river.

So we handed in our hateful grey uniforms and went off to the naval base at Kiel. Officer cadets were embarked in three training ships, *Gorch Fock*, *Albert Leo Schlageter* and *Horst Wessel*, lovely white swan-like things each of 1,000 tons. They were just my idea of the old clippers I used to read so much about. I never doubted that I would last out the course, for, after all, my whole boyhood had been spent sailing.

Cutters ferried us over – I had been drafted to the *Gorch Fock*. Petty-officers divided us up at once into port and starboard watches and we were allotted our lockers and hammocks. At our first muster the Captain, a pale-faced, lean creature, addressed us like this:

"You have the honour to learn your seamanship on board this fine ship. Don't imagine simply because you've done some preliminary training in Dänholm that you are useful seamen. You have a great deal to learn, or rather you have everything to learn that a naval officer needs to know. Whatever advances may be made in warship design, ships will still be manned by seamen and not by specialists. You're going to have a hard time here and will often curse the harsh service, but you'll come to look back on your early days in the *Gorch Fock* as a happy memory. Show yourselves worthy of the man who gave this ship her name and his life for people and Fatherland at the Battle of Jutland. Dark days lie ahead. Only those who work with heart and soul will be fit for the duty they're called on to perform. I want you to wear your blue uniform with pride and see that you do honour to it."

We were dismissed and fell in again, for now the duty officer had some pointed words to say. Last of all, a leadingseaman addressed us. He was tall and thin with an angular, lanky figure. But he was an experienced first mate in sail. "We used to have wooden ships and iron men. Now we've got iron ships and wooden men, and we've got to get back to where we were as far as the men are concerned. We're going to make a start at it here and now."

By this time everyone had had his say and we had to fill our lockers. How small they were, only $1^1/_2$ x $1^1/_2$ x $1^1/_2$ feet! But we managed it in the end, hard as it seemed – every handkerchief; even our comb had its allotted place.

I had great difficulty with my hammock, as once I was in I could move neither arms nor legs. I didn't know then of the little wooden wedges that old sea dogs insert between the cords at either end to keep them apart.

Hands were called at six o'clock every morning. Turn out, lash up and stow. The hammock, made of sail canvas, had to be rolled into a sausage-shape so that if need be it could be used as a life-buoy. It was a matter of moments, for in ten minutes we fell in on the windswept upper deck in sports rig for PT.

March 1940 was a particularly cold month, and the thermometer seldom registered anything above 10 degrees below zero. An hour before reveille the boatswain's mate on watch always filled the buckets with cold water. We had to break the crust of ice by thrusting our heads into the pails. Then, stripped to the waist, we scrubbed ourselves down with soap while the wind went howling through the rigging to remind us, and we were never allowed to forget it, that we were on board a sailing-ship. Next we had to shave on deck, though later on we were allowed to do that in the washroom. We learnt to do things the hard way. The slightest lack of keenness was punished by orders to go up aloft, up foremast, mainmast and mizzen, up one side and down the other, with nothing on but shorts, and of course with no gloves to keep our fingers warm. We were never allowed to wear gloves when we went aloft, so that we could get the feel of the rigging in our finger-tips. There were all sorts of other rules, but it was all quite different to our training on Dänholm island, for we were really learning seamanship now. All the knowledge that we acquired on board was vital for the safety of a sailing ship at sea. You would hardly expect me to enjoy freezing on deck or aloft, but I soon began to feel that all this was an essential part of a naval officer's training. I enjoyed it all much more than I had enjoyed my time on Dänholm. The whole atmosphere was different. I would often remember the time when my master in the schooner of which I was boatswain had seemed so exacting, but it was child's play compared with this life which I had undertaken of my own free will, to learn what it really means to go to sea, as compared with travelling around in liners fitted with central heating.

The German Merchant Service also maintained two sailing ships for training. Their crews were taught the job the same way as we were, so it seemed to me that these methods really must be essential to a naval education. My companions shared my view, and in general there were very few who revolted against the life.

So it was that we learnt the essentials of seamanship, knots and splices, boat-pulling, reading a compass and taking bearings. Above all, we learnt mast-work, to go and come down from aloft.

Now I must confess that the last time I stood looking up at the tall masts of the *Gorch Fock* I was not a bit happy. They were about 125 feet high, and when you were standing at the foot of them they looked higher still. We could all swarm up the rigging together as far as the mainyard, both sides of the mast at once, for the lowest shrouds ran up the masts themselves. But then came the tops, and after that things began to look difficult, but it was amazing how quickly we got used to it. When we were off duty for short spells we had a chance to put in some extra practice, and we got so used to climbing up and down that in the end we could do it with our eyes shut. It was a stirring sight when we all went up in our white uniforms and manned the masts and spars.

The beauty of a sailing-ship lies not least in her being spotless from stem to stern. Every object aboard is absolutely clean, the metalwork shines and sparkles in the sunlight from endless polishing. The deck, which is regularly sluiced down and holystoned, is so clean that you could eat your meals off it. An enormous quantity of soap is used to keep things spick and span. As for our uniforms, we changed them every other day.

There was an auxiliary motor for generating electricity, and another, which served as auxiliary engine, which I never knew to be used. Sails were set and furled by hand, and the anchor was weighed by hand too. In a dead calm we brought the ship back to port by our own muscles. We would lower and man a cutter, with an anchor that weighed a ton in the sternsheets, and row about 500 yards towards our objective. Then we would heave it overboard. The anchor to which the ship was lying was then hove in with the hand-capstan. All this usually took a quarter of an hour, with accordion accompaniment. When the anchor was away the ship would be kedged by the hand capstan to its new anchor berth. There was always keen competition between the watches, and the victors were rewarded with an extra rum issue at tea or with special leave.

I spent three months in the *Gorch Fock*. We soon got to know each other very well, and even the officers would confide to us their personal and family worries. On one occasion the rudder needed repairs, underwater. I volunteered for the job and went down with a diver's helmet on. After that, for all the rum I drank, I collapsed with a fever. There was not much room in our sickbay and every cot was occupied because so many people grazed their legs running up the masts, and those injuries were just the ones that took longest to cure, especially when complications set in. At first I thought they were going to send me to hospital ashore, a prospect which I viewed with dismay as I did not want to part from my friends, but luckily there was an empty officer's cabin aboard and I was allowed to occupy it for a week. The cabin was centrally heated and furnished in dark heavy oak, which was frightful. But I had my own wash-basin with running hot and cold water, and even a bell to ring for the steward. It was a temptation to ask him to bring me a cocktail, but thank goodness I never did! What I really did enjoy was when a petty officer knocked at the cabin door to ask to speak to his superior. Our regulations prescribed that they could only come into the cabin when the answer to the knock was "Come in"' But if you said "What do you want?" they told us from outside. At first I always said "Come in", and they would spring to attention with the thumb behind the seam of the trousers before they began to speak. But when they recognised who I was, as they were bound to sooner or later, then you should have heard their language. Still, there was nothing they could do about it except walk out of the cabin again, for they couldn't mete out any punishment for my impertinence, no knees bend, no spell at the pumps, since I was on the sicklist and not to be disturbed. But they often went out with the parting words "Well see about this later". However, in ten days I was back on duty.

Three times a week we had shore leave. In the evenings on the lower deck we used to foregather and sing shanties, the officers joining in, for despite the strict discipline we were a real community.

At the end of our three months in the *Gorch Fock* we were confirmed as naval cadets. As such we wore a star on our sleeve encircled by a twisted golden cable. Apparently I had proved myself satisfactory on the whole, although I had not been quite smart enough in matters like heel clicking and saluting. Still, I didn't worry about that, for the main thing was that I could now proceed to the next stage of my training.

Early in May 1940 I was appointed to the battleship *Schlesien* in the Baltic. The deck was by no means up to *Gorch Fock* standards. Our quarters, and indeed every spare inch of space, we shared with cockroaches. Every sailor in the world knows these creatures, and simply has to get used to them. Only in U-boats were we spared these and other such vermin. I lived in number three turret, where thick iron armour plating without scuttles shut out the view; instead we had two 15-centimetre guns right on top of us.

The *Schlesien* had seen service with the High Seas Fleet before the First World War. She had four 28-centimetre guns in two twin turrets, and was obsolete by modern standards; but she was suitable as a training ship for this very reason. On board her, for example, everything could be worked by hand, and this was put to good use. My own action station was in turret "Anton", the foremost one on the fo'c'sle, down below in the magazine. We tried our best to have a nap behind the huge shells and cordite cartridges, but, when we were caught, the punishment was made to fit the crime. The shells, which weighed a hundredweight, were loaded into the lifts by hand and then delivered electrically up to the gunhouse. A special grab was used for transporting them, which was worked by four men, and we had to watch out in case, as sometimes happened, a shell slipped out. Woe betide him who had his foot in the way! We were using practice ammunition only at this stage.

By comparison with the others manning the 16-centimetre guns we were considerably better off. We never had to work faster than the lifts and the gunhouse crews could handle the ammunition, since for drill purposes the charges and projectiles were loaded into the gunhouse and then sent back for the process to start afresh. But things were quite different at the 15-centimetre guns. They had to drill with a specially-designed "loader", where the projectiles were loaded and rammed home until they started to fall out of the fore end, which meant that you could drill at any speed you liked, and if one gun hotted up the rate of fire all the others had to do the same.

As a punishment, flag "Luzie" was often used, the blue-white-blue signal flag which meant shifting one's uniform in the shortest possible time. For hours on end, sometimes, we had to shift from blues into whites, and into the various rigs from "night clothing" to "steaming kit" with everything fully packed. That meant more work in the evening, for if everything wasn't spick and span by the next morning they would think up something else, and the variations were endless. Boat-pulling was quite often practised; old battleships' cutters are particularly large, and the oars long and thick. We often returned to the ship with blistered hands.

In the *Schlesien* we travelled all over the Baltic, training in gunnery and in general concentrating on alternate theory and practice. We carried out firings, first with aiming-rifle tubes in the guns at iron targets, then with sub-calibre ammunition at longer ranges, and finally with full-calibre. A battleship is a world of its own, and it is amazing how everything goes on with absolute precision and how everybody fits into his place. It takes a year at least for a battleship's complement to be properly trained and fit for action, which is not surprising when you consider that the *Bismarck*, for instance, carried a ship's company two thousand five hundred strong. While we were still learning our job in the *Schlesien* great things were happening in the world. So far the war had barely interrupted the training of new entries. True, during the campaign in Poland the training-ship *Schleswig Holstein* had bombarded the Hela Peninsula, and in April 1940, when we were still aboard the *Gorch Fock*, the Norwegian campaign had transformed the naval situation. Yet it hadn't interfered with our own training.

But on 10th May the campaign in the west began. In a single astonishing sweep German troops crossed the Meuse and the Scheldt, and Dunkirk became a symbol for the flight of the British Expeditionary Force. Paris fell and German soldiers appeared on the Atlantic coast. Many of my companions were afraid the war would end in victory before they saw active service.

One day we were issued with rifles, hand-grenades and service kit, with a view, apparently, to being embarked next morning – as we thought, in preparation for a landing in England. Rumour followed rumour. Three days passed, and no transport turned up. We had to hand in our gear, only to get it back, again to no purpose.

What was the matter? What plan had our leaders in mind?

After an impatient wait some of us got orders to join the 16th Advanced Flotilla. But first it had to be formed in south-west France, so we went to a naval camp at Wesermünde where a large force was mustered. Here, just after the Armistice had been signed with France, we piled into motor buses, about a hundred to each bus, and drove first across Germany and then in the wake of our army through Belgium and France. It took several days and we had a chance to see those countries and their peoples with our own eyes, and above all to observe the aftermath of everything that had just happened. We travelled through country that had just been fought over, with carcasses of dead animals strewn everywhere, glimpses of burnt-out tanks, and streams of prisoners of war and of refugees who had fled from the invading German Wehrmacht, which they had been taught to think of as a horde of barbarians. And now they were streaming back to their homes.

That was our first experience of the horrors of war, and it shattered our youthful self-confidence as we rattled down the highways I couldn't help thinking of my father, who had served in 1914-18, used to say there is no greater evil and no madness worse than war.

And yet I couldn't help thinking it wasn't going to be so bad this time. How much quicker, how much more decisively things had worked out in France compared with those nerve-racking, hard-slogging battles of the First World War! And hadn't the misery and the casualties on both sides in the west been far less?

The mood of the French population seemed to bear out those surmises. On the surface they weren't unfriendly to us. At any rate we often enough heard their abusive, "*Ah, les Anglais*' accompanied by significant gestures.

On our journey through France we slept in various billets. Once we had to take over a barracks that had been a hospital. It was in a frightful state, filthy and overrun with vermin. But eventually we reached the area of La Rochelle without incident. The crews of our flotilla were mostly fishermen in uniform with very little training, who seemed best fitted to man fishing smacks and such like craft and convert them into fleet auxiliaries.

Our officers had orders to act with humanity and consideration when they requisitioned French ships, and we did indeed treat the defeated French with kidglove methods. How the propaganda, put out later to the contrary, distorted facts. For instance, we had to convert a 1,500-ton Cross-Channel steamer built in 1898 into an armed auxiliary cruiser, though a ship of the latest design lay nearby. We certainly had to pay in German sailors' lives for this chivalrous behaviour!

Our own service conditions had changed overnight, many of our officers being reservists and ignorant of how cadets were trained, which was not such a bad thing for us. As it is much easier to get out of military habits than to get into them, we soon grew moustaches and whiskers, took the grommet out of our caps and let our trousers go baggy. Our cadets' stars, of which we had once been so proud, had long been fitted with press-studs, for we didn't feel it absolutely essential to be conspicuous everywhere as embryo officers. Officers often went around in plain clothes, but we were forbidden to do that.

Work on the future auxiliary cruiser was going ahead fast in the dock at

La Pallice. As I had studied French eight years at school I was made an interpreter, and often had to go round with the Flotilla Commander and take part in many conferences and negotiations with Frenchmen. We had plenty of festive celebrations too. Nobody took the war seriously any longer. We were on the threshold of peace – or such at any rate was the general opinion.

Our first task was to convoy merchantmen through the Bay of Biscay to Germany. We often detonated mines, and were seldom attacked by English planes.

Shortly afterwards I was transferred to a 250-ton patrolboat. We had one gun and a crew of twenty, and as often as not had to lie off various harbours in the Bay of Biscay letting heavy seas break over us. At first I was terribly sea-sick. My fishermen companions took a fiendish delight in my condition, and when I turned as white as a sheet one of them in a Hamburg accent suggested the best thing for me was a tot of rum, of which I was induced to drink a large glass. It was hardly a success.

In fourteen days, however, I found my sea-legs as well as any of them and I have never been troubled since.

Once, while I was in the patrol-boat, an Italian submarine was torpedoed before our eyes, and we had to escort it into Bordeaux, depth charges being dropped all around us. Our supporting ships were not properly equipped for this kind of warfare, and anti-submarine devices cannot be improvised. On the other hand, we were seldom attacked by aircraft, for in those days the Luftwaffe controlled the Bay of Biscay.

Everywhere we found preparations for the invasion of England. All available shipping was being adapted for it. Auxiliary motors were being put into river-boats and, to increase speed in an emergency, one or even two aeroplane engines installed, while the bows were cut away and a collapsible ramp fitted to land tanks on a flat beach. Everyone was working frantically. We too had rifles and hand-grenades aboard to be ready to go into action any moment. Again we really did seem to have got that far. Then one day there was really tremendous excitement in the flotilla – all ships received sealed orders to be opened at the code word "Sea Lion". We could be pretty sure that the order to attack England was contained in them, together with the course and landing points. As the days went by, every conversation turned on this topic.

But, as it turned out, we had striven to no purpose. Before very long we learnt that the undertaking was abandoned. Had our leaders got a better plan?

Our unit had nevertheless proved itself worthy. We were awarded the minesweeping and patrol badge.

Subsequently we had to put into Rotterdam for a refit, and within a few days we cadets were told off to report at the Naval Academy at Flensburg. Our heads high, our first war decorations on our swollen chests, we marched through the gate of our future home. Our whole term met again, friends gathering in from all the fronts – the North Sea, Norway and the Mediterranean.

The Commanding Officer, a forbidding-looking Admiral, vented his wrath on us, however, at the first inspection. We were far too unkempt; gone to pieces, in fact. Some had grown beards, others were content with embryo moustaches. Certainly no one could recognise in us the former cadets on board the *Gorch Fock*, or the *Schlesien*. Some of my term-mates had been killed, and many others were unrecognisable. Almost all were somehow changed. Action had turned them into men.

The school buildings formed an enormous stone maze. Four shared a bed-sitting-room. The lofty corridors were lined with memorial tablets and model ships, while ancient tattered flags decorated the walls. Irreverently speaking, it literally stank of tradition. Actually we were now only half-way to being midshipmen; the sword-belt, emblem for having passed the last officers' exam, was lacking. But who knew that ashore?

At the Naval Academy we had to work hard, for the authorities were exacting. The main thing that we had to master was astronomical navigation. We learnt a great deal about higher mathematics too, and were also taught physics and chemistry; the standard of instruction was excellent.

Of course the German Navy sets great store by practical experience. So we learnt how to sail a boat and bring a motor launch alongside. We also went out on instructional cruises aboard the 1,000-ton steamer which was at our disposal, but we had comparatively little training for active service, though we were coached in the general principles of gunnery and torpedo. There were so many different types of ship, and so many new weapons always being produced that it seemed unnecessary to learn everything in detail, even if we had had the time to do it. There was so much to learn that it would have taken whole decades to master it all and by the time a pupil had got to the end he would have forgotten the beginning. So the Naval Academy at Flensburg just gave us an overall course in navigation and a general education in tactics, weapons and naval history.

Midshipmen are well known for their escapades, and our superiors didn't take them too seriously. One of my friends bought a fishing-rod, line and tackle and spent his free time fishing off the pier. He came in for a good deal of chaff, as it was a well-known fact that the waters round the Academy were quite devoid of fish, but the amazing thing was that his first day's catch weighed close on 20 pounds of very fine fish indeed. Word went round very quickly, and even the officers took an interest and came down to watch. He never failed to catch something, and when they saw his fine catches many other people bought rods and lines to try their luck. My friend just beamed with pleasure. Apparently he was the only one who really understood fishing, having been, as he explained, on a minesweeper up the Norwegian fjords, where he had acquired his special knowledge. You had to get the feel of the thing, he told us, and there was a good deal more to it besides. Nobody took that seriously, but there was no getting away from the fact that he was always successful and we never had any luck at all. Then one day, when there were quite a number of anglers gathered on the pier, he began to pull up his rod with a great show of effort, telling us that he had felt something particularly powerful tugging and we must expect a quite exceptional haul. How right he was: he had actually caught a filleted herring. We all shouted with laughter, and it was a wonder that he got off that pier alive after the number of times he was ducked. The explanation of this extraordinary phenomenon was that he had an accomplice, sitting right under the landing-stage with a sackfull of fish bought from the fishmonger, hooking a fish onto his line whenever he dropped a pebble through the boards, the shape of the pebble standing for a different sort of fish. Our comedian had to report to the Commanding Officer, who, however, appreciated the joke and didn't inflict any punishment.

Another time the duty officer was asked for leave for a hearse with a coffin in it to drive through the grounds. All the permits were checked and apparently in order; the only thing was that there seemed to have been no previous notice given. However, it was eventually allowed through.

It so happened that my class were just having a lecture from a civilian instructor called Peter. "Come in," he growled in what he imagined to be a suitably nautical tone of voice – he was most anxious to got a reservist's commission. Slowly the door opened and, a solemn voice murmuring "My heartfelt sympathy," a big black coffin was brought in by four bearers in deep mourning. They laid it at the foot of the instructor's desk and vanished in a moment, but not before the solemn voice had spoken up once again, this time to announce, "This is a coffin for *Herr* Peter".

The motor hearse had driven off at top speed, but the coffin stayed, to the fiendish glee of all present except *Herr* Peter. He dismissed the class at once in fearful dudgeon and proceeded to lodge a complaint with the

Company Commander. This was just the behaviour so typical of him that made him so unpopular. Anyway, there was an official enquiry, but although the whole Naval Academy was questioned and the undertaker traced, the culprit was never discovered. After the coffin had been paid for, it was presented to a church, and that was the last we heard of the subject.

We also had boxing, fencing and riding lessons, great importance being attached to physical courage. Unfortunately my boxing instructor was unlucky because we had a young champion doing the course. He was a heavy weight and the instructor, who was a light-weight, had no idea what he was up against. "Boxing," he told us in a short preliminary speech, "is the best test of a man's character. Never show fear, which is a contemptible emotion, but go right in and all out. Now, if any of you have had any experience of boxing, come on and try your luck."

We formed a ring and they set to. The instructor hit his opponent hard on the nose, then the cadet went for him for all he was worth. He was twice the weight of his opponent and had arms like a bear. Before the first round was over the fight had to be ignominiously broken off.

After fifteen months I went on leave for the first time, home to my parents in Berlin. As naval uniforms were rare in the capital people thought we were something very special. The Army and the Luftwaffe almost always addressed us as "*Leutnant*" because we wore a type of small shoulder strap, but in front of hotels we were taken for porters and on the railways for stationmasters. Once when I was waiting for a train on the Underground a lady addressed me like this: "Forgive me, *Herr* stationmaster, but could you tell me the quickest way to get to the Wannsee?" A short way off a naval Captain was walking up and down. "Excuse me, madam," I replied, "I'm new to this station, but you see that gentleman with four gold rings on his sleeve, he's been here a long time and will certainly be able to help you" – and made myself scarce before the storm broke.

Our time at the naval college was coming to its end. We had passed our last exams and received our longed-for sword-belts. After a farewell dance we were returned to active service, myself with two of my companions being appointed to a U-boat. In this early May of 1941 the Reich was not yet at war with the Soviet Union and no open hostilities had so far broken out against the United States. The immediate task ahead was our fight against English seapower, and for this there was no doubt that our most potent weapon was the U-boat.

With the contemptibly small number of submarines – twenty[1] perhaps –

[1] Publisher's note – The actual figure was 57.

which we had when the war began it had been impossible to take on what was then the greatest sea power in the world. But the ship-building programme, embarked on when England declared war in 1939, must have shown results by this time.

It was a strange feeling to start in on this new and active phase of our lives, and all our conversation turned on what lay before us. I had read a number of books about the First World War, and remembered the declarations of Allied statesmen about how close to disaster England had been brought by the German U-boats. Apart from many warships, our submarines had had over 18,000,000 tons of merchant shipping to their credit between 1914 and 1918. I called to mind the names of Weddigen and of other successful U-boats commanders like Arnauld de la Periere and von Spiegel, whose lives I had read. During our instruction time I had always thought of existence on board a U-boat as of something uncanny and mysterious. These must have been real men, waging their own kind of war under water, out of the light of day, in foul air and oil-soaked clothing. And these men had once again earned the respect of the whole world by their exploits. But we knew that many boats had not returned from their operational cruises. It was just two months since the boats of three of the most celebrated had been lost – U-47, *Korvettenkapitän* Prien; U-100, *Korvettenkapitän* Schepke; and U-101, *Kapitänleutnant* Kretschmer. The last-named alone had lived to tell the tale – and he was a prisoner of war.

CHAPTER THREE

THE GREY WOLF SHOWS ITS TEETH

IN DANZIG lay our U-boat. We could hardly wait to go on board, for no one outside the ship's company, not even officers of other ships, were allowed aboard a U-boat. Top secret! Under no circumstances must the enemy obtain the slightest information about a weapon that was so dangerous to him.

At the naval school we had been issued with completely new gear – new uniforms, fresh linen and, among other things, a vast quantity of starched collars. We also had a sea-chest each and two smaller trunks. We were somebody now and no longer went around with kitbags.

At last after a long hunt we found our ship. It was painted grey and barely distinguishable from the mole. Two sentries were on guard, one on deck and the other on the pier, carrying automatics and by no means smart by parade-ground standards. When we asked if the Commander was on board they said he had just gone ashore and wouldn't be back till tomorrow. It was useless to explain that we must come aboard, at least to stow our gear. There wasn't a hope – unless we produced a special permit from the Commander. Orders from the Naval Academy were not enough.

However, we had learnt that nothing was impossible and didn't give up so easily. After a long search we found the senior watch-keeper in the depot-ship, who, after all, gave us our permits. We had brought all our gear from the station and now tried to get it on board. The petty-officers all grinned. We were their equals in rank, but that meant nothing, for we had never seen a submarine and were completely dependent on them. Before long we had got our light luggage into the control-room all right, but the sea-chest just would not go down the hatchway.

"*Achtung!*" The ship's company stood to attention. We saw a white cap, the emblem of a U-boat Commander – it was an unwritten law in submarines that he alone could wear that headgear.

"Are you cracked? What do you want with all that rubbish aboard? Get your gear into the depot-ship and report to me in my cabin in half an hour."

When we got back he addressed us something like this: "You are just nobodies aboard and absolute good-for-nothings. The most junior hand knows more than you do. You are simply ballast and useless wasters of air, so don't forget it. Your job is to get used to things and pick up knowledge. In three weeks we go on operations; don't imagine I'm going to take you if you aren't up to your duties. Remember you have the honour of serving in the finest and most decisive arm of the German Reich. Our life is hard and exacting, but we bear it gladly for love of our Fatherland. Take as your examples the U-boat aces of both wars and try to imitate them. If you put all your heart into the service, in the end you'll knock yourselves into sailors."

We were issued with two sets of grey-green overalls, one leather outfit, sea-boots, two pullovers, six sets of underwear and six pairs of stockings. Except for our linen that was all we were allowed on board; besides, there was no room for more in our lockers. Everything else, even our blue uniforms, we sent home.

We had to move around in a very confined space and settle ourselves in among a bewildering array of instruments and apparatus. Every pipe had its purpose. We had to find out where it came from and where it led to. To make our instruction as thorough as possible we were made to crawl around under the plating, clean out the bilges and do the foulest jobs imaginable. Our fine midshipmen's uniforms were forgotten, and we never wore badges of rank – instead, each in turn, one of us had to share quarters with the crew, one with the petty officers and one with the chief petty officers. By turns also one of us would eat in the wardroom.

Our ship was the usual operational type VIIC of 600 tons surface displacement, and at that time carried a complement of forty-two. The smaller 250 ton U-boat was not really up to long-distance service out in the Atlantic, where we had the advantage over the heavier 800 ton class in being more easily manoeuvrable, quicker to dive and, above all, better equipped defensively, being harder to locate.

A U-boat looks outwardly like a cigar, but its living vitals are concentrated in the inner pressure hull, where the engines, motors and batteries are to be found. But since this pressure hull is heavier than water and by itself would sink to the sea-bed at once, buoyancy has to be provided by means of an outer hull. By this means its cubic capacity is increased without adding proportionately to the total weight. The space between the hulls is used to carry the fuel and also the ballast tanks filled with compressed air that makes the whole so buoyant that when surfaced about a seventh of the pressure hull is raised above water-level.

When it dives this buoyancy is eliminated by flooding the tanks up to a predetermined level. If the boat remained stopped, it would sink to the bottom, because in actuality there can be no "suspended ships" such as one meets in ghost stories about ships which have disappeared. The boat can only be held at the requisite depth by the use of engine speed in conjunction with the so called "hydroplanes" – broad vanes on each side on which, when tilted upwards or downwards, the flow of water acts in order to steer the boat towards or away from the surface.

And now let's make a tour from stem to stern. We start with what is called in German naval parlance the House of Lords (*der Pairskammer*). This is derived from the nickname "Lords" given to seaman ratings in the Navy. In the fo'c's'le are ranged four torpedo-tubes, and in every tube there is normally a torpedo already loaded; four more are stowed under the deck-plating and two others over them protected by wooden planks. The crew sleep in collapsible bunks, always in two tiers, three "Lords" to two bunks. Other members of the ship's company share the twelve bunks in the fo'c's'le, normally the torpedo and wireless ratings. Then there are the engine-room ratings' officially styled "stokers". Two stokers to a bunk. It works out all right in practice because so many ratings are always on watch. As soon as one turns out, another lies down in his bunk, so that the bunks are never cold, and it's all rather like an industrial town with a housing shortage and dormitories occupied in shifts.

But that doesn't leave us free to sleep between watches. Everyone, naturally, must be present at mealtimes, when a table is brought in and the upper bunks raised so we can sit on the lower ones. Besides, the crew must keep the ship clean; hands have to be detailed as "cooks of messes" to serve and clean up after meals.

Next to the fo'c's'le is a mess for the chief quartermaster and the two engine room artificers. On the port side a refrigerator space, and opposite it a WC, or "heads". Next comes the wardroom for the two upper-deck officers and the chief engineer – at one end of it the Commander's cabin, which is only a corner of the wardroom shut off by a thick curtain.

The Commander, of course, must be at the centre of things. So the wireless operator's cabin is opposite it, and next to it a cabin with all the vital instruments for underwater navigation, hydrophone gear and the like. Next to the Commander's cabin is the switch-room – and then you get to a place whose importance its name expresses: the control-room.

Here the Commander and chief engineer get together when we dive. Here, too, all the apparatus in use when dived, such as hydroplanes, pumps, etc., is to be found. It also gives access to the conning-tower. The control-room lies amidships and can be shut off from the fore and after ends of the boat, its bulkheads being tested to a water pressure of 600 feet. (The cabin bulkheads can only take a hundred feet).

Next comes the petty officers' mess, with eight bunks which have to be used by turns – astern on the starboard side the galley and another "heads". Finally comes the Diesel engines adjoining the electric-motor room, with the after torpedo-tube, and one spare torpedo under the deck plating.

In 1941 every new boat put to sea with a crew half composed of men with operational experience and half of recruits. Every other man in our ship's company wore the U-boat badge and the Iron Cross second class. Our Commander himself, a tall, fair man with a striking, angular face and clipped speech, had been through a whole series of operational cruises as senior watch-keeper.

The six-month training period, which every boat had to spend in the Baltic, was nearly over by the time we were appointed as midshipmen. It consisted of tests of many kinds which were carried out in special flotillas. For example, breakdowns in the engines, lighting and other departments were caused purposely by experienced engineers in accordance with actual incidents reported by boats which had returned from operations. Work had often to be carried out in darkness, and in fact when it came to an emergency the lighting was usually the first thing that went. If a boat passed these tests, there was no more training, but if not – back to school. We got through ours successfully, until only the final tactical exercise remained. This was considered most important, lasted fourteen days, and represented a hard test for a boat and its crew. When I did one later as a senior watch-keeper, the training-unit lost two boats out of twelve – and two others returned to harbour damaged.

These tactical exercises were on a grand scale, covering a wide sweep of the Baltic. Once the surface-ships had taken up their stations we behaved exactly as if we were out on active service in the Atlantic. There would be a large, strongly escorted convoy zig-zagging along its course, with at least fifty planes patrolling the area to report every U-boat sighted.

We no longer used the usual practice-torpedoes, which differ from the real things only by the absence of a warhead charged with 200 kilos of explosive, and which are set to run deep so as to under-run the target. Now, we signalled the torpedo firing settings to the target-ship so as to establish whether we would have hit, and consequently to enable us to correct our errors. Previously, the target-ship had been able to mark the traces of our torpedoes at night by means of a lamp fitted to them, and by day through the bubble-traces.

We got through it all with fairly good marks and then proceeded to Kiel to be fitted out for the real thing. The whole place here was humming with activity, at least ten boats lying along the U-boat mole, all alike, grey and very long for their beam, about 150 feet from stern to stem, their youthful crews burning with idealistic confidence. I ran into many friends here from the Naval Academy, for every boat carried three midshipmen. Young officers had to learn their jobs at sea, and the price in losses had to be paid. No submarine training-school could give us the experience acquired on active service.

Lorry-load after lorry-load of ship's stores came alongside, until we had food enough to last three months without going short, for our rations were far above those in any other branch of the service. We had to stow our stores according to plan, and distribute then evenly about the ship so as to keep trimmed when dived. Secondly, the stores must not shift when diving, which can easily happen at a diving-angle of 60 degrees. Thirdly, the provisions must not hinder the service of the engines or block the gangways.

In the latter years of the war every boat was issued with the same storage plan. Hams and sausages between the torpedo-tubes and in the control-room, a three weeks' supply of fresh meat in the refrigerator and new-baked bread to last the same time slung in the fo'c's'le and in the motor-room. When the fresh food ran out we lived entirely on tinned foods.

We secured at a special pier to embark torpedoes. First we loaded through a special hatchway for'ard and then through another aft. The arms embarked included 8.8 centimetre and 2 centimetre shells, and an impressive number of machine-guns and cartridges for our automatics. On the upper deck we had a gun specially designed for U-boats and an automatic AA gun, while if need be a machine-gun could be brought up from the conning-tower. Eventually our equipment was complete, the oxygen cylinders filled, the air-purifier renewed. We had despatched the last mail to our families, and were due to sail at dawn.

The Flotilla Commander gave us our farewell address: "*Kameraden*, you must realise that you are serving in the finest and most effective service of our dear Fatherland. The destiny of our fellow countrymen lies in your hands. Prove yourselves worthy of your trust. We know no fear. Our motto is 'Go in and sink'."

The coast of Germany is far away. Our Commander has decided on the Iceland passage to the Atlantic between Iceland and the Faroes. In the First World War, also, the greatest problem of the U-boat Command was precisely this of getting ships from the coast of Germany to the Atlantic. Without the use of the French coast we had no direct access to our operational areas. The Channel is too easily guarded; being so narrow, it can be blocked by mines and anti-submarine nets. But despite its greater area the enemy had command of the north-west passage round the British Isles as well, and ships with new entries in the crew had to face a stern test in the first few days. Lack of experience among new entries would often account for relatively high losses in the first operation. Besides, many were seasick, and your seasick man is unreliable both on watch and when diving.

I am on watch Stern look-out, just like an ordinary seaman. For'ard stands the officer of the watch with a boatswain's mate and a couple of ratings, and a midshipman as well. For four hours, with no overhead cover or any other protection, come rain, storm, or snow, each of us has to keep watch over his own sector with binoculars or the naked eye. For four hours the same monotonous sequence – glasses up to sweep the horizon – down to wipe them clear of pray, then up once more – an unending ritual. Woe betide the man who falls asleep or relaxes a moment. It may cost his own life and the lives of the whole ship's company.

Four days at sea have passed, with nothing in sight, neither plane, nor ship, nor floating mine. We are running at 14 knots. The long slender boat cuts like a knife through the swell – no ordinary wave can make her pitch. As it is, heavy seas are pouring over the upper deck to break against the conning-tower, sometimes sweeping over it and pouring down on our heads in a cold douche. A porpoise! For a moment we enjoy the distraction. How quickly it can move! More quickly than we can. Oh, what does all this war talk amount to? We haven't seen a thing. Anyhow, the English haven't enough planes to be on guard everywhere at once. That's just a leg-pull from the old hands, trying to frighten us,

"Aircraft 040 degrees," reports the boatswain's mate. The officer of the watch looks up.

"Stand by."

Fit to wake the dead, bells jangle all over the ship. We all jump to diving stations. The most intimate activities even in the "heads" must be interrupted, whatever the state in which a man has to show up. The watch on the bridge leaps down the hatchway, hands and feet on the steel ladder. You simply drop down – but watch your step or the next man will be on top of you, and sea-boots can be hard. In five seconds you must close the hatchway. One and one fifth seconds for each man. You must just get down somehow. In the control-room a man stands by to help you up if you fall.

The Diesels are stopped at the alarm-bells and the engine-room springs into feverish activity. The motors are coupled up and air-intakes and exhaust-valves shut off. Each man knows his job – the reward of countless exercises. Red lamps indicate every essential detail, to guard against mistakes. The whole boat senses danger – the alarm-bells don't ring for fun. No order to flood yet?

Clank!... the hatch shuts. "Flood!" shouts the officer of the watch, his legs dangling as he throws his whole weight on the wheel which seals the hatch shut.

"Flood!" orders the chief engineer, standing before his flooding-table, where all the section indicators have lit up, showing "Ready to dive" on each dial. "Five, four, three, two – both." This means the diving-tanks, which are numbered from forward to aft. Men jump like cats to the valve-levers, twist them open and repeat "Five, four, three, two both." Now again we can see the justification for all our interminable practice – for a false move can mean death. All goes well, and lamps indicate that the diving-valves are open. Water rushes into the tanks, and the boat dips her bows – 10 degrees – 20 degrees.

"One!" orders the chief and the vent of the after tank is opened wide This is left on purpose until the last, so that the diving-angle can be much sharper. The electric motors are running at full speed, although all you hear is a slight drone. The whole boat vibrates. "Diving tanks open," the engineer reports. "Five fathoms... Eight... She's diving fast.... Ten fathoms."

"Sunderland flying-boat on the port bow," the officer of the watch reports. "The sky's overcast, and the plane's dived into a cloudbank. It wasn't coming our way. Perhaps it hasn't spotted us. If it has we shall be 26 fathoms down before the first bombs drop."

"Twenty fathoms, ship diving fast, 35 degrees load."

"Down to 50 fathoms!"

A distant boom filters through to us. It's nothing like an artillery explosion on land. Rather it's a kind of dull crackle. Water's a good sound-conductor, and down here we might be cooped in a floating drum. But no one says a word, no one stirs. Each man has his station and mustn't budge

– it might upset the trim of the ship. At last the reports ring out, "All clear for'ard! All clear aft! All clear control-room!"

There's to be no attack, then. The explosions are a long way off.

"The boat's on an even keel now close all vents."

The last vestiges of air must now be driven out of the corners of the diving-tanks, as they can he awkward when running dived. At great depth the air is compressed, and the additional Water makes the boat noticeably heavier, while at shallow depths the opposite is the case, not to speak of the bubble, which can move forward and aft just like a spirit-level, causing constant changes in trim. Besides, these make a great deal of noise, and are altogether a thoroughly unpleasant feature.

We all feel better again, knowing that in emergency we can blow tanks without leakage of air and loss of surfacing effect. God help the boat whose vents get damaged by bombs, and then jam.

Five minutes pass and still nothing happens. The engines are running at slow speed. We can stay like this two days without showing ourselves. Still, it's not our job to skulk about dived but to attack and destroy.

The Commander has retained a healthy respect for bombs from his own early days. You've got to experience them to know what war means – there's nothing worse for a new ship's company than the first weeks without air attack. Carelessness, a false sense of security, can be fatal. So for an hour we lie dived. Then:

Commander: "Up to periscope depth."

Officer of the watch to engineer: "Up to periscope depth. Half speed ahead both."

Engineer to hyrdroplane operator: "Both hydroplanes hard up. Flood 50 litres.',

The water-pressure decreases as the boat rises to the surface, and she expands slightly, thus becoming more buoyant, which requires counter-flooding, and an experienced engineer knows just how much is necessary. It depends' among other things, on the salinity of the sea-water in the area. The Commander is in the control-room, ready to have a first look-round through the periscope. There's no hurry: the great thing is to catch the boat at 20 metres and trim her off so as to hold her at periscope depth of 14 metres without any oscillating. That is most important' since the periscope must only just show above the surface, and the motors must run dead slow so as not to leave a propeller-wake or a streak of bubbles behind the periscope itself.

Now we must have our nerves under firm control, or, best of all, forget about them altogether. You've got to become a robot, identifying yourself with your boat which takes on her own kind of life. At depths below 100 fathoms a U-boat starts groaning and creaking – when she surfaces she shakes herself like a dog. In bad weather you can hear her groaning like one of our look-outs. At 50 fathoms she's content, cutting through the water calm and silent.

At 20 metres the Commander seats himself at the periscope: a mechanical work of art, trained left and right by means of pedals. The right-hand controls an angling mirror which permits vision from 70 degrees above to 15 degrees below the horizontal. The left-hand operates a compensating lever which allows for the motion of the sea and small movements of the boat itself. A handle controls the lenses, giving an alternative magnification of 1·5 or ·6, with various degrees of shading against glare. In addition, a Kontax or cine-camera can be used with the periscope. The whole can be warmed, so as to prevent misting of the mirror, Obviously, the view through the periscope includes crosswires, rangescale, and bearing from a compass-repeater, while a glance upward or downward enables gunfire to be controlled with the aid of various graduated dials. The figures are coloured red, green, yellow, black or white, corresponding with the type of information they give. A torpedo firing-push is close by.

Near the periscope is the main attack-table. This was standard during the war all over the world, and may well have caused considerable astonishment, and justifiably, after the capitulation, when our enemies were able to have a look at it. It is not just a normally-geared calculating apparatus, but a triangle-solving machine with various graphs and cams, which is coupled up directly to the periscope. This made it possible to fire at five different targets in a convoy within the space of a few seconds, and without having to alter the original estimates of the convoy's course and speed, etc.

The Commander has taken a careful look-round with the periscope, searches the sky, which seems clear, and gives the order to surface. The diving-tanks are accordingly "blown, and when the engineer reports the conning-tower hatch as "free", the Commander swings the wheel over, springs up on the bridge, and together with the officer of the watch anxiously scans the sea and the sky. Meanwhile the boat has risen further, with the electric motors still running at full speed, which would enable her to dive in the shortest possible time in emergency. There is nothing in sight. As the Commander gives the order "Blow through the electric motors are stopped and the Diesel exhaust gases are led into the diving-tanks to expel the last remaining water. This has the advantage of saving compressed air and of helping to preserve the tanks themselves from corrosion. The watch takes over on the bridge, and the boat settles down to normal surface running, to the monotonous hammering rhythm of the Diesels.

In those days we often had to dive to escape bombers, and they never harmed us. Also, we saw many floating mines. Once indeed we surfaced to find a mine wire stretched diagonally across the conning-tower. It was very rusty, and luckily the mine had come adrift. "We shall meet in the rose garden, you and I," was one of the love songs we used to learn in Middle High German lessons at school – I suppose it was with this in mind that our U-boat crews used to call the mine-sown area "the rose garden".

Once we sighted a fishing-boat. The general opinion was that we should send her to the bottom, for she was in forbidden waters. But the Commander was against it. She was too small, it would be a waste of a torpedo; besides, it would draw attention to our whereabouts and in a few hours submarine chasers and planes might be on top of us. It's not worth that risk, to sink a fishing-boat. After all, a U-boat costs four million marks.

So at last we've got through the Iceland passage, and are lying in the area designated for U-boat operations. There's a sort of U-boat belt here, the units stationed at various distances from one another. (The German Intelligence Service was largely responsible for these dispositions – it wasn't pure coincidence that U-boats so often happened to be right in the path of a convoy.)

"Mast on the starboard bowl".

The look-out is on his toes. We can only make her out dimly through our glasses, but when the Commander comes onto the bridge, he spots it at once – it takes long practice and experience to pick things out like that. We novices can hardly credit it.

The Commander tells the chief engineer that he wants to bring the boat closer.

"Hard a-port, half-speed ahead both."

In the interests of low fuel consumption one Diesel only has been running at slow speed. Every four hours we have been switching engines to give them equalised running-time, and thus keeping them tuned up and ready for any emergency. We've been cruising hitherto at 6 knots, but now in a few seconds we increase to 12, altering course until the mast lies right ahead.

"Steady as you go!" the Commander tells the helmsman.

The next thing is to mount on the attack-sight the extra-powerful telescope used for surface attack, which, like the periscope, is directly connected to the range-finding apparatus. When we dive this extraordinary telescope can be left on deck without anyone worrying, and can stand up to a pressure of 100 fathoms.

The Commander's on to it now, the mast at the centre of the cross-wires, but growing smaller and drifting to port.

"Heading for the States, evidently," he mutters, "but not an American, I hope. These are forbidden waters. Neutrals should keep to the sea-lanes and not zig-zag. We'll soon find out."

The blowers are started. Air is being drawn into the shafts by the supplementary pumps. The bows lift, and white foam is streaming past on either quarter. We can still only just make out the mast through the attack sight.

"Hard a-starboard!"

We're at right angles now to our former course – the masthead's vanished.

"Steady on 20 degrees to starboard."

Slowly it swings back into view and grows larger, and – as we again increase our speed – eventually settles down to a uniform size, indicating that we are following the ship's course all right. No! She must be faster than we are, for the mast is drawing ahead.

"Damned fast ship. Hope we get her."

We're all on our toes and ready for action stations. If we are only a knot faster than her it'll be hours and maybe days before we can attack: that is, assuming the enemy doesn't zig-zag much and no planes appear. You need a good deal of luck to torpedo a ship from a position astern. Once more we increase our speed till we are doing 17 knots, the engines warmed up now and their exhaust barely visible. The engine-room personnel are working magnificently. The masthead is staying the same height, so the ship must be travelling at just about 17 knots too.

"Damned fast. "Full speed ahead!"

We can still go to emergency full speed, and we have our electric motors as well. With our reserves of power we must be able to make it. Luckily we haven't got the sea right ahead, and, as usual, only spray splashes over us, the grey wolf being so lean. The propellers are turning at 360 revolutions a minute. A streak of foam trails in our wake – a sight that's the terror of all merchant ships, but a fine one for us.

For two hours we maintain full speed. If we only had unlimited fuel we could keep this up for weeks, for the engines (M.A.N. type) are up to it. Before she goes on active service every ship has to run at full speed for eight hours, and these engines seldom give out.

The plot is being kept in the control-room. Every five minutes the Commander shouts down the bearing and distance of the ship and the chief quartermaster plots our course and our enemy's. Every zig-zag is noted. The ship keeps up its speed and zig-zags continuously, but we know her mean course, and can relax, even though the masthead is actually lost to sight now and then, every hour we check her position. All's well. It's really just like manoeuvres in the Baltic. At 14 miles' range the mast will be visible, but we are still 16 miles off. Everybody's on edge. Shall we catch up with her? It's certainly a change from our monotonous lives of watch-keeping, torpedo drill, mealtimes, cleaning ship, and then more eternal watching. The torpedo officer checks all torpedoes – unnecessarily, but it's better to make quite sure. The Diesels, each with its eight cylinders taller than a man, keep up their regular hammering. The indicator needles are carefully watched; water and exhaust temperatures mustn't rise too high – not above danger level. So far everything is under control, and we have only been at full speed for four hours.

It is five in the afternoon.

"We're not making much headway,', the Commander grumbles. "We must attack after nightfall. No use chasing her for another day – using up too much fuel. By tomorrow at 5 a.m., when it starts to get light, we must have fired our torpedoes."

All the upper-deck officers and the best look-outs are on the bridge. They have no reliefs, and all they get to eat and drink is special U-boat chocolate and coffee, so as not to make too great a call on their strength with the effort of digestion. They've got to keep their eyes open. Only one cup of coffee at a time gets taken up to them, so as not to distract more than one of them at once. There's no talking – there's nothing to talk about anyway.

Twilight falls... in twenty minutes it'll be dark, for it's eight o'clock already. To keep contact at night we must close to 3 miles. The moon shines through the clouds and it is growing steadily lighter. That is good for us in one way, for we can pick out an object 4 miles away, but it is bad for our gunnery as we can't approach closer than 5,500 metres, for fear that the enemy may spot our white bow-wave and wake. The sea is gleaming with phosphorous, giving the effect of little sparks flying into the air.

"Object ahead!" The Commander spotted it first. All our eyes light up with excitement. "What a stroke of luck! She's right ahead and 4 miles off."

By now it is exactly ten o'clock. It'll take nine hours to manoeuvre into the correct firing position, but at 5 a.m. it'll be steadily getting light, and before dawn the torpedoes must be out of their tubes...

We can only make a guess at the position of the ship, for we dare not let her catch sight of us. But we can increase speed. Down goes the engineer to the engine-room – before long we're going all out, the white spray splashing over our conning-tower. Up on the bridge the watch are drenched to the skin, for nobody thinks of putting on oilskins at such times. All our blowers and compressors are screeching for all they're worth – we keep on blowing our diving tanks every five minutes, for we have to keep as high above the waterline as we can, since the higher we are the faster we go. True, the increase in our speed's only fractional, but it is an increase. We're all keyed up for the chase and the odd thing is that nobody has time to feel afraid, though we all know there'll probably be at least two guns mounted on the stern of the ship we're after, to say nothing of machine-guns and automatic weapons, for every ship that doesn't travel in convoy carries a whole armoury. One hit from any of those guns would cripple us when we came to dive, and that would mean the end. A hit on the Diesel tank would be enough to finish us too, for it'd be sure to leave a long oil-slick in our wake which would make us a sitting-bird target for any U-boat chaser that came along.

It is 4 a.m. at last, and now instead of getting darker the opposite is happening – we can distinguish the sky from the water-line. At five sharp we must fire; it'll be our last chance.

Fifteen minutes to go, and everyone is at their post – two men are operating the range-finder – one in the conning-tower, one in the control-room. The torpedoman and petty-officer torpedoman are at the for'ard torpedo tubes and there is another torpedoman aft. All this time the Commander is leaning against the rail at one corner of the bridge, his binoculars glued to his eyes and his long fair hair and beard hiding his face. He is like a being possessed, caught in the grip of our frenzied manhunt.

"Tubes one to five ready!" the torpedo-officer's shouting the tubes are wet and their outer doors open. Meanwhile the engineer is reckoning the quantity of water we'll need to have in our tanks to correct the boat's trim after the torpedoes have been discharged. All five of them are ready in case we need them.

"Tubes one to four – ready for surface fire," comes through the speaking-tube from the fo'c's'le, and from aft: "Tube number five – ready for surface fire. Bridge control!" Torpedoes can be fired from several positions, from the fore and after compartments, the control-room, the conning-tower and the bridge. The order passes to the control-room and the switches are made. Dim white lamps in the conning-tower show the petty-officer at the range-finder that the order has been correctly carried out, and he reports to the torpedo-officer, who in his turn reports to the Commander.

We're still moving parallel with the enemy and slightly before his beam. The attack-sight is "on", with the target in the centre of the crosswires.

"Target Red 90, speed 16½ knots, range 7,000 metres, torpedo speed 30 knots, running depth 7 metres." Our torpedoes are set to run at a depth of 7 metres below the surface, to pass about 2 metres beneath the target. A magnetic pistol fires the charge, which blows in the keel plates and causes the ship to break up.

During the First World War they had to aim with the whole boat, since after leaving the tubes the torpedoes continued on the same course as that of the U-boat, under the control of their gyroscopic automatic steering-gear. Attacks were difficult under these conditions, particularly when destroyers and other convoy-escorts had to be avoided. But in the Second World War our new torpedoes could take up a course automatically up to 90 degrees away from the direction in which they were fired – the latest models even up to 180 degrees. The chances of success were in this way considerably increased, since the boat was no longer committed to a fixed course during an attack.

The torpedo officer at the attack-table reports "Lined-up", and the switch is made by which the attack-table is connected with the gyro-compass and the attack-sight. The mechanism churns round and two red lamps indicate that the process of calculating the information which has been fed in to it is not yet completed. The lights go out after a few moments, and the petty-officer at the attack-table reports the resulting settings to the torpedo-officer. From this point onwards our own alterations of course are of little importance, being allowed for automatically. The target must simply be held in the crosswires of the attack-sight in order that the apparatus can do its job. The torpedo-officer gives the order "Follow" to the attack-table. A lamp glows, and the attack-table is now controlling the binoculars on the bridge. Meanwhile the constantly changing firing-settings are being transmitted automatically to the torpedoes and set on their angling mechanism. With this system we can fire at any moment and on any course, provided that the 90-degree limiting angle is not exceeded. The torpedoes will run to a pattern that spread over roughly a ship's length by the time they reach the range of the target. We turn to our attacking course.

We can now see the enemy clearly – a British tanker of 18,000 tons.

We are doing 12 knots and the range is now 5,000 metres. The torpedo petty-officer at the attack-table reports the settings to the torpedo officer whenever they alter, and the Commander is listening in.

Commander to torpedo-officer: "Fire at 4,600 metres. Aim at her foremast." And then: "Rate of turn, red 3."

This is the speed at which the boat swings when the rudder is put hard a-port. Our new torpedoes, combined with careful judgment of the moment to turn, which is helped by the attack-table, allow us to turn away before firing, which not only saves time but enables us to fire at shorter ranges.

Torpedo-officer to torpedo petty-officer: "Red 3. Stand by for surface fire."

Commander to helmsman: "Hard a-port."

Torpedo petty-officer to bow tubes: "Stand by for surface fire."

The acknowledgment comes back: "Tubes one, three and four ready."

Commander to torpedo-officer: "Fire when ready."

Torpedo officer: "Ready."

Torpedo petty-officer: "On – on – on." By this he indicates that the change settings are being accurately transmitted to the torpedoes as the boat swings.

The torpedo-officer at the attack-sight is holding the ships foremast in the crosswires... "*Fire!*" and he presses the firing push. "*Fire!*" repeats the torpedo petty-officer, and the torpedo gunner's-mate at the fore tubes hears the order through the loudspeaker system, he has a hand on two of the firing levers and a leg across the third, in case of a failure of the remote-controlled firing-gear. The boat shivers three times in succession and three short heavy hissing sounds are heard – the noise of the compressed air by which the torpedoes are discharged. Firing is "staggered" at 1⅕ second intervals to prevent mutual interference between the discharges. At the order "Fire", the Chief floods to a prescribed amount in order to compensate for the weight of the three torpedoes – for the boat must be ready for an instantaneous crash-dive if necessary. The Commander looks at his wristwatch – fifteen seconds running time yet.

Boom! "Hurrah! hit!" The Commander at the periscope is the only man who can see anything. He switches his microphone in to the general loudspeaker system: "Hit aft; stern seems to be buckled!" The magnetic pistol has worked well, it appears.

Her wireless is still working, however. An SOS goes out on the 600 metre wave-length. *German submarine* – with our position.

"Very good'" remarks the chief quartermaster; "it's friendly of the English to give us an exact position. No more need to worry today."

She's no longer moving through the water and is giving off steam. Rudder and steering apparatus seem to be damaged. We attack again. It's easy now, for we are just over a thousand metres away. They've spotted our periscope, though, and with all their machine-guns and quick-firers let fly at us, endangering the periscope glass. We attack from the other quarter and dive under the ship at 10 fathoms. The hydrophone – operator reports:

"She's right overhead!"

In a submarine attack the Commander controls the ship, gives the target information and fires the torpedoes himself.

The torpedo-officer only sees that the proper settings are put on the attack-table. This time we are going to fire the stern tube, which we don't often get the chance to use.

"Range 100 metres . . . fire!"

The roar's terrific. We've fired from much closer this time; underwater the noise is frightful. The tanker has broken in two.

Everyone has a look through the periscope. The fine ship before us is sinking into the sea. Emotion overcomes us. The demonic madness of destruction that becomes law the moment a war breaks out has us in its grip. Under its spell as we are, what else can we do? Lifeboats and rafts are meanwhile being lowered, those aboard saving themselves as best they may. We can't help without running into grave danger, and in any case we've no room aboard – U-boats are built to allow space for the ship's company and no more. The enemy is well equipped with life-saving gear and these men on the tanker will certainly soon be picked up by a warship.

At first we allow ourselves a litttle relaxation, if you can call it that. Cruising at our depth of 95 fathoms we put on some gramophone records and listen to the old tunes that remind us of home. As a special surprise we get a glass of brandy. The ship's company have been long unused to that, as spirits are normally forbidden at sea. It's hard for smokers too – you can only have a cigarette on the bridge or in the conning-tower when surfaced.

The next job is to load the reserve torpedoes. For an hour and a half we all set to with a will in the hope of scoring another success. We're altering our position too, for our victim has had time to send out a wireless message and it is highly improbable that any more merchant-ships will pass through this area. More likely submarine chasers and planes.

By this time half our fuel has been expended. In such circumstances U-boat Commanders would be left free to alter their area of operations as they saw fit.

We might bag another ship in the next few weeks. But for a long time we had been living out of tins – in fact we felt like tinned meat ourselves. Ashore they call it claustrophobia, but there at least you have a better chance to shake it off than in our cage Always the same faces, the same uniforms, the same round of duties, with not the remotest chance of privacy; every idiosyncrasy, every weakness served up on a plate for our companions to observe. The way the next man will react, the motions he'll go through when he puts his clothes on and eats his food known inevitably in advance. Sometimes we were driven nearly mad by knowing what one of our beloved messmates was going to do for the umpteenth time. The very food tasted of U-boat; that is, Diesel oil with a flavour of mould. The moment the cases were opened the foul air streamed in and gave our victuals their typically U-boat taste. The bulkheads sweated, every single thing turned mouldy. Leather outfits and shoes went green in a fortnight if we didn't use them.

As it was, we got orders to put into Lorient, which we did crossing the Bay of Biscay surfaced by day and dived by night. Faces brightened up. Everybody looked forward to his mail, for at last we should be able to write home. Nobody there would know if we were dead or alive, since Naval HQ only posted us missing when we were six months overdue.

What was more, we got air cover, and with Messerschmitt fighters flying round us we felt that nothing could go wrong now. It was fine to feel relatively safe again. We went into dock with white pennants showing the amount of tonnage sunk fluttering from our periscope. (If we had sunk a warship we should have hung out little red flags – the U-boat arm had already acquired its own traditions and ritual.) We put on clean clothes, the same uniform grey, needless to say – the ship was grey and we were grey. Several officers from the base were standing on the pier, and a band was playing. And – were our eyes playing tricks on us? Could we trust them? – girls, real live girls, even though they were cipher officers! With such a reception our hearts jumped for joy.

The Commander made his report to the Flag Officer, and after an exchange of salutes we were dismissed. The girls gave us fruit and beer. Good beer, too. If we didn't exactly get drunk we certainly were not unaffected, having been so long unused to the good old sap of barley-corn. Then we just fell on our mail. It was a wonderful moment when we tore open the letters from home. Not only that, but we found all the clothes sent from home set out in order. A good thing too, for we could hardly go ashore in our U-boat kit reeking of oil. We meant to go out dancing again, to enjoy the pleasant things of life. The last weeks had been much too grim.

The second evening after we put in there was a party on board, to which everyone came from the Commander down to the most junior rating, our Moses. All differences in rank were forgotten, and we sang and drank, and laughed together, even one or two over the eight not being taken amiss The famous "beer report"[1] was gone through. We midshipmen all got a rocket, and rightly, for it was our first voyage and we had made many mistakes. While keeping watch on the bridge one had reported a seagull as a plane, and when the alarm-bell rang another had put down his cigarette on deck instead of throwing it overboard. A doggerel verse warned him to take care and not to jump into the sea instead of down the hatchway next time. Even the officers, including the Commander himself, weren't spared.

The C-in-C submarines, Admiral Dönitz, came aboard. It was the first time I had ever seen at close quarters the man whose will-power and planning had made our arm the terrible weapon that it was.

"Men of the U-boat fleet," he said, "you have done well on your first operation. Though we have few submarines in service you may be sure we shall soon have more and will be hard on the heels of our enemy. We shall cut the life-lines he depends on for his survival. The course of this war depends largely on you. Already our sinkings have outstripped his capacity to build. It is our aim and object to see that no enemy ship dares show itself upon the seas."

Before us all, drawn up on deck, the Admiral pinned the Iron Cross first class upon our Commander and various veterans among the crew. Others got the Iron Cross second class. Ratings who had not got the U-boat badge received it now, for we had been at sea longer than the nine necessary weeks and had been successful into the bargain. The Admiral thought it all right for the first voyage, but next time we must do better. He shook hands with all the ship's company except the midshipmen.

"You have still to become U-boat men. You've set yourselves a great task."

I can't say I was particularly pleased.

A third of the crew were on leave, the others had to get on with their routine duties, which was not much fun considering we had been on duty all the voyage.

A U-boat rest-camp at Lorient was the chief attraction for us. This fine building had a swimming-bath, and we could play table tennis and billiards, and occasionally see films and go to the dances held in it. Apart from some dubious night haunts it provided the few diversions to be had there.

[1] Traditional German naval ceremony.

CHAPTER FOUR

"Go In And Sink"

THE weeks before our next operations were spent at Lorient. The war had entered a new phase. The Eastern campaign was in full swing and a vague hope stirred in all of us that this eastward switch might bring a rapid, decisive result. England, however, must feel relieved. Together with Rommel's men, we of the Navy, particularly the submarine branch, were the forces on which the island kingdom and her friends the Yanks, obviously growing less neutral every day, would now be able to concentrate their strength.

We had painted an enormous 'V' on the conning-tower. I don't know just why our war leaders had seized on that letter for propaganda, but for us it was the symbol of success. *Veni, Vidi, Vici* (We came, we saw, we conquered). We midshipmen meanwhile had got so used to life aboard a U-boat that we were attending fewer lectures now, but of course we still had a lot to learn, for you never really master all there is to know about a U-boat.

Our destination this time was mid-Atlantic – we had already crossed longitude 15° W, beyond which point the wireless was generally silent. This meridian was, so to speak, a frontier, and we generally referred to waters west of it as our "Western zone" after we had crossed it we received an increase in pay. For days on end there was the same monotonous routine; nothing different ever happened, and we began to long for something to turn up. At last there came an urgent signal, which the wireless operator laid before our Commander – it was news of a convoy.

It was still far off but coming our way, if it didn't alter its course, and we proceeded at half-speed towards our interception point. We should have sighted it in two days, but still we saw no smoke. However, it must have been a very important convoy, for the High Command sent us out a reconnaissance plane although we were 8,000 kilometres from the nearest airfield. A U-boat is a small object to make out, however, and we were doubtful if it would find us. The wireless operator tried to make contact so as to give him our exact position and, if possible, our bearing, but this wasn't an easy job, for aeroplane transmitters are not powerful.

We kept on sending out signals at short intervals, and in the end it all worked out amazingly. The plane came into view, a BV 138 built by Blohm and Voss for special tasks, and we flashed the probable position of the convoy. The BV flew away. Two hours passed, and we went ahead without any more news. Our Commander personally had not much faith in radio. Although under favourable conditions European transmissions can be picked up in America, messages from ships can normally only be picked up 20 miles away.

In the end our BV 138 returned, and flashed this message: *Convoy. Square* 10. *About* 50 ships escorted by 10 destroyers. We went full speed ahead, with the whole watch standing by, the petty-officer torpedoman checking up on his torpedoes, and the plane still flying over us. At three in the afternoon we sighted the first column of smoke. Then another, and a third. We sped ahead. Next the first masts showed up, more and more of them.

"Why, it's a whole forest," said someone on the bridge. "We've certainly got a job."

"Stop chattering and get on with your work, the Commander snapped back, without lowering his binoculars. The BV 138 made off, wishing us luck, and vanished.

"Those airmen don't have such a bad time. Home to mother every night. I wouldn't mind being in their shoes."

We sent out a twenty-word signal – position of the convoy, course, speed, strength and escort – so as to put High Command in the picture. Every two hours we transmitted fuller details. We were the first U-boat to contact the convoy and our job now was to call in all other U-boats in the area, that being the whole point of our wolf-pack tactics.

But I do not mean to imply by this that we were all acting under a unified command. United action in the Battle of the Atlantic merely meant calling up all available forces, for once in touch with the convoy every ship acted on its own, yet in this way we could annihilate convoys of fifty ships and more in actions that went on for days.

The night, which was pitch dark without a moon, was in our favour. But some U-boats were failing to show up. As far as we could judge from the reports we got we might be six in all by dawn. It was an important convoy – fifty ships with war materials bound for England.

"Make call-signs," the Commander ordered.

Rather a nerve, sending out wireless messages right in among the enemy ships. If our wavelength was known we were finished. But it couldn't be helped, we had to have more U-boats.

Wireless operator to Commander: "U X has contacted the convoy."

Next thing we learned was that another of our boats had done so too.

So we were now three in all, and our Commander decided to attack. Bearing indications to the other ships were no longer required, as you can see the flash of a torpedo miles away, and if one ship went up in flames it would light the way for the other U-boats. We wanted to torpedo four ships, so we picked out the big ones, preparing to attack the furthest first and the rest afterwards, allotting two torpedoes to the largest ship, and one each to the others. If possible all four must hit simultaneously, so as to leave no time for alterations of course. We were quite close to the nearest ship already – 650 metres perhaps.

"*Fire!*"

The ship throbbed five times – we were using our after tube along with the rest. In fifteen seconds the torpedoes should hit. We grew impatient; they seemed such very long seconds. Perhaps the tinfish hadn't run properly. Was anything wrong?

A spurt of flame and then two thuds. Sound travels through water faster than through the air. One more explosion aboard the same ship. She was breaking apart now, and in a moment she had gone down. There could be few survivors. Then came two more explosions – one torpedo had evidently missed. In a moment the convoy which had been peacefully pursuing its course sprang to action with much flashing of red and blue lights and signals to change course. The British knew their job. To handle blacked-out ships in convoy at night is no easy task, yet there was no collision. A pity for us, it would have saved us extra work.

The destroyers now pounced on their prey. Searchlights switched on, guns opened fire, depth charges detonated. But we were not discovered, for we were still in among the convoy, which was probably the last place they expected to find us. Instead of making off or diving we went further in. Our Commander guessed they'd overlook us there, and he was right.

With a small range of vision you can easily overlook a submarine from the high bridge of a merchant-ship. It's hard to make out that dark streak on the water, to distinguish it from the shadows cast by the higher waves.

The rear doors of the torpedo tubes swung open, one torpedo after another sliding in. The crew were bathed in sweat, working like mad. It was a matter of life and death, no time or place for reflection. If they found us now we were utterly lost, for without our torpedoes secured we couldn't dive. This was war – "Go in and sink."

It lasted thirty-five minutes. Already we were making ready for the next attack.

Torpedo control officer to Commander: "Tubes one to four ready!"

Heavy explosions. Ships were breaking up, others letting off steam and coming to a standstill, thick smoke mounting skywards. Searchlights played on the dark water and the starry blaze of oil. SOS calls never stopped going out on the 600-metre wavelength. More U-boats were coming up. Still more explosions.

'Hope we don't buy one of the 'overs'," said the second officer of the watch. "It would be the limit if our own people sent us all to hell."

And it might so easily happen, seeing that we were all mixed up with the escort ships.

At last the convoy was really breaking up, ships making off in all directions. That was bad for us for we could only take one target at a time now. Besides, they'd had their warning – some were zig-zagging, others steaming on a circular course.

Hard a-starboard. Our next victim, an 8,000-ton ship, was held in the crosswires. "*Fire!*" Almost simultaneously with this fresh command a flash went up from her. But we only scored one hit, though she was listing heavily aft.

"Object ahead!"

We tried to get away – but the object moved more quickly than we could. Gradually it loomed larger. "Watch out! They're after us!" As we rushed below we heard more explosions. We were just robots. Things were happening spontaneously, events taking charge of us.

Our High Command had warned us about fast launches shipped aboard the convoys and launched when U-boats attacked at night. Their strength lay in their small size, amazing speed and strong armament of quick-firing guns. You could only see these craft when they were right on top of you, if you saw them at all.

Down to 50 fathoms. With 40 degrees load and all our power we sank into the depths... Was our engineer by any chance related to a fish? He dived the boat to the exact depth, put her on an even keel, closed the vents and finally reported "All clear."

"Well done," the Commander congratulated him.

Our friend the enemy had always got a new card up his sleeve. Well, the war would be very dull if he hadn't. Anyhow, we'd know better next time. The watch on the bridge were pretty alert in my opinion.

The first depth-charges were exploding now, but a long way off. We were still too close to the convoy and the destroyers couldn't pick us up because of all the other din – a happy state that could hardly last long. The Commander gave the order to proceed at silent speed. The electric engines were almost inaudible, and the auxiliaries shut off; words of command whispered, the ratings went around in felt shoes. Everybody not needed for immediate duty went off to lie down, as in that way, we expended less oxygen. Nobody knew how long we would have to survive on what we had and you consume less lying down than standing up and talking.

The convoy was steaming away now, its propellers barely audible. But three destroyers were after us, and before long the sound of their Asdic, like fingernails run over a comb, grew all too familiar. Another of their Asdic devices rattled like peas in a tin, a third screeched like an ancient tramcar taking a curve. We weren't likely to forget this experience. I thought of the man who went out to discover what fear meant. He should have been there.

The destroyers surrounded us, their explosions sounding closer and closer, usually in threes. My action-station was cramped up aft at the speaking-tube, and every time a charge exploded I had to report if there was any damage. The tube ran between the hull and the torpedo-tube, and in this minute space I had to support myself leaning on one hand and aching in every limb. There was an almighty roar, and the boat sank like a stone for 20 metres: the light went out, and the emergency lighting came on automatically. It was no joke, when the enemy had us held like this on the dials of his instruments. Engine-noises got louder – and the depth-charges ever nearer. The electricians were moving about the boat repairing damage: meanwhile the lights were switched over to the second of the two ring-main electrical circuits with which the boat was fitted. It went on for hours. Our wireless operators maintained contact with the destroyers, and kept the Commander posted; when they came closer he went to the wireless-room himself to give orders. Every time a destroyer was on top of us we altered course – you have to react instinctively. Fortunately our Commander knew exactly what he was about. He betrayed no feeling, and indeed everyone gave an appearance of self-control, but we were all uneasy, myself not least. It had never been as bad as this – we couldn't see, we couldn't shoot, we just had to last it out, though it was almost more than we could stand. We counted sixty-eight depth-charges.

How long could this unreal combat, not man to man or even weapon against weapon, this inhuman strain go on, this mixture of luck, blind tactics and instinctively doing the right thing at the right time? We were caught up in a mechanism, everyone getting down to their work in a dead, automatic silence. There was something uncanny about the whole atmosphere aboard. The ratings looked like phantoms.

There is a frightful crack, just as if the boat has been struck by a gigantic hammer. Electric bulbs and glasses fly about, leaving fragments everywhere. The motors have stopped. Reports from all stations show, thank God, that there are no leaks – just the main fuses blown. The damage is made good. We are now using special breathing apparatus to guard against the deadly carbon-monoxide which may be in the boat. The rubber mouthpiece tastes horrible. This is war all right, real war, not a film-war of waving flags and blaring music.

Yet the instinct of self-preservation is active in every man of us, and if we had been asked if we really felt frightened I doubt if we could have given a plain yes or no in reply.

The hundredth depth-charge bursts. Beads of sweat stand out on every forehead. As our last hope we discharge the *Bold* – the Asdic decoy to which so many U-boats owe their survival, its chemical components creating a film which hangs like a curtain in the water and gives an echo like a submarine to the destroyer's Asdic.

Our tactics then are to turn, intentionally, broadside on to our hunters' so as to make sure they get our echo' then turn away sharply and show them our stern, sneaking away and leaving the *Bold* for the hunting pack to worry.

Our *Bold* evidently helped us, for fewer depth-charges were exploding now, and it did seem the enemy had been tricked. After counting one hundred and sixty-eight charges in eight hours, we at last began to breathe again. The destroyers were steaming away. They had to pick up their convoy, for it needed an escort for the coming night. If every U-boat had pinned down three destroyers, then only one of the ten could still be with the convoy, and things would be easier for other U-boats.

Our kind of warfare is not what the layman thinks it is, just slinking up under water, shooting and stealing away like a thief in the night. On the contrary, most ships are torpedoed in an escorted convoy by a surfaced submarine; and although the size of a destroyer doesn't allow for an unlimited number of depth-charges – I imagine that they must make do with about eighty – what they have can make things hot enough while the action lasts.

We waited for an hour and then we surfaced.

Full speed ahead.

The batteries were then recharged, which was the chief thing, for without our batteries we could not dive and in effect would cease to be a submarine. We reloaded our tubes and once more we were ready for action, only a bit worn out. I remembered our training-advice on Dänholm: "No sailor gets worn out – if you can't keep your eyes open jam matches into them." Instead of matches we took cafein and pervitin tablets, which wasn't ideal for our health but we had to go without sleep for days and just could not do without them.

That night we failed to overtake the convoy, and reported our success to date to headquarters: four ships sunk, 24,000 tons in all.

The Admiral replied: Not 24,000-36,000. The, *ship were...* and he listed them. *Well done. Go on in and sink the rest.* Our intelligence service was superb, and this time they had decoded the enemy wireless signals. Altogether 100,000 tons had been sunk, and we hoped that there was something left for the following night; we had already forgotten the counter-attack with depth-charges, and counted on the destroyers having exhausted their supply, But in fact we found ourselves unable to keep up with the convoy, for our fuel was almost exhausted and we had to turn back to base. Later on we learnt that the convoy had been almost annihilated.

Mast in sight – another ship. Her course made it possible for us to attempt an attack, for all our lack of fuel. We went in as night was falling, in spite of the fact that a destroyer was making straight for us. Just then, however, we spotted a red light and altered course It was impossible for the destroyer to have sighted us – besides, surely it would have opened fire?

Crash dive!

No depth charges. Was it sheer coincidence? We surfaced. The destroyer was still making for us. Again we saw that damned red light.

Crash dive!

It happened three times, and by the end of it we were all worn out.

Later, we should have dived yet again when we were attacked by two Sunderlands sighted too late when they were already too close to us. So far we had had no engagement with planes, though an automatic 2-centimetre gun was mounted aft on the conning-tower for such an emergency, with one magazine always ready and another to hand. The Commander now wanted to close the hatchway, but it jammed – a spring had given when the destroyers depth-charged us. Meanwhile, a Sunderland was flying towards us. Making his mind up in a moment the Commander rushed up the conning-tower, took his station by the gun and fired.

The distance must have been over 1,000 metres. The plane sheered off, yet by doing so it couldn't have made a worse mistake, for now it exposed its whole length of fuselage at close range without being able to use its armament. After another burst it suddenly dived and dropped into the water. Then the other attacked, and the Commander again opened fire. One of its engines burst into flames and it flew off. All this time the engineer was working feverishly on the conning-tower hatch, and at last we were again able to dive. Everybody congratulated the Commander for his marksmanship. But for his presence of mind and speedy action we should all certainly have been killed.

Later there was a wireless broadcast about our Commander and he was awarded the Golden German Cross.

This time we put in to Brest, a larger base than Lorient. We were quartered in the naval college, an imposing building on a hill-top visible for miles around, beneath which, in the cliffs, the first U-boat pens were being constructed: formidable armoured underground wharves and docks. Air attacks were becoming more frequent and we didn't want to let up on our U-boat attacks at any price through delays from ship refits. The work went ahead at an unimaginable rate, unending streams of lorries with sand and cement pouring through the streets. The workmen were quartered in new housing-estates, and it was altogether a masterpiece of organisation.

No one knew what was to happen to the midshipmen. Were we going to Germany to be trained as watch-keeping officers or to be sent on some other course? We hoped not, for we felt it was high time for us to be given some responsible post. One thing was clear, and that was that alone of all the ship's company we were not getting any leave, which was honestly a bit much after our second operation. Instead, we were sent to a U-boat rest-camp – all very fine, with a white sandy beach and facilities for every sort of recreation, but small use to us when we wanted to see our families. We had so much to tell them, and what can you say in a letter? Meanwhile our ship was being fitted out for another operation, so it looked as if we were to go out in her once more.

After every operation all Commanders had to report in person to the C-in-C submarines, and by so having the chance of expressing their points of view and suggesting improvements helped to keep the High Command in direct touch with ships on active service. Working on the principle that experience is acquired at sea and not round green-baize tables, we avoided a lot of useless correspondence which generally holds things up because a host of intermediaries write minutes and feel it their duty to make comments.

This time our Commander came back in a bad temper. He had reported the red lights and expected to be listened to, but Admiral Dönitz seemed to attach no importance to them and belittled our Commanders report, attributing it all to the effects of strain. Why he did so we had no idea, but could only presume that at another level things take on a different perspective. However much we might grumble we had to obey our orders, and to hope that the High Command had a broad view.

Three cheers! The midshipmen were going back to Germany for further training. What is more, we had eight days' leave to fill in the time before our next course. I went to Berlin, where my mother wept for joy to see me. The thought of my being in submarines was alarming to her, but I have an idea she was proud, all the same. Meanwhile the war in the East was going well. With few exceptions the people at home were convinced that we were going to win. Of course, they had the oddest notions of submarine warfare, how could it be otherwise?

We always scored our greatest successes at night, surfaced, for then we were almost invisible, much faster and more manoeuvrable than when dived. But if by any chance the enemy were to discover a device to make us visible in the dark our potentialities would be distinctly reduced. That red light was the beginning of a fateful process for us – the possibility of making an object visible in the dark with infra-red rays was evidently being exploited. Our losses at any rate were increasing perceptibly compared with the year before.

A large percentage of the fellows on our present six-months' course were my year, but many others of my contemporaries had been killed. We learn't now all about the latest torpedoes and the way to use them. We tested out what we learnt at target-practice, going on to study for the wireless officers' exams and practising the various coding procedures and operational signals. After that we went to a U-boat school, where we were taught how to go alongside and dive, underwater navigation, methods of attack, and all about the interior of a submarine. In spite of all our experience on active service we had a great deal to learn. Anybody who first looks round a control-room is overwhelmed by the multitudinous shafts and wheels, whose bewildering array is liable to turn even engineers, from other types of ships, pale. We wound up with a course in gunnery, working on the 8.8- or 10.5-centimetre guns in the bows of our little training-ship. This proved the most popular part of the course and we enjoyed it thoroughly.

We had now passed all our tests and the course was over. Our eagerly awaited promotion to sub-lieutenant *(leutnant)* and our appointments to sea followed. My boat belonged to the familiar VII-C class, and I reported to her Commander at Danzig. This time I knew what to take aboard and had left my sea-chest comfortably at home.

The boat had just been built, and had begun its trials in the Baltic. After four weeks my Commander took me aside to congratulate me:

"A friend of mine has asked for you as watch-keeper, and the U-boat Command has sanctioned the appointment. Tomorrow we shall return to Danzig and take over our new baby."

Almost at the same time as I took up my new appointment I was promoted lieutenant *(Oberleutnant)*.

Our superstructure rose high above the waterline, a sign that there was a good deal still missing from her refit. The crew, who gave a first-rate impression, half of them having seen active service, drifted in by twos and threes. All day we crept around our "embryo".

"You must get to know your boat thoroughly before you can handle such a masterpiece of technique," the Flotilla Commander had warned us.

At last we set out on our tactical exercise – to attack a convoy crossing the Baltic heavily escorted by aircraft and destroyers. All this absorbed an enormous number of U-boat officers for a single exercise, but it was probably better than losing untrained crews on active service.

It was pitch dark, we could hardly see the horizon, cloud and wave merging into a single oppressive dark-grey mass, through which our boat, dark grey itself, moved indistinguishably from its surroundings, its main strength lying in this very chameleon-like quality.

Fire!

Our gunnery was perfect, almost too good for practice. Then came an emergency signal:

> *General. Break off the exercise immediately. Switch on VHF R/T.*[1] *UX rammed and sunk. Try to contact. Watch out for survivors. Lower all lifeboats and pickup anyone you find. Flotilla Commander.*

Parachute flares shone through the night. Searchlight beams from more than ten U-boats, destroyers and ships in convoy criss-crossed over the waters, all in direct communication with each other, just as if they had been linked by telephone. The lives of fifty men were at stake, The Commander, one officer and three ratings were in fact shortly picked up. They said that

[1] Very High Fequency Radio Telephony – the main fleet intercommunication line.

while cruising surfaced they had been rammed by a dived U-boat and sunk at once. The five survivors were standing on the bridge so they were able to jump into the water.

Our wireless operator soon told the Commander he had contacted the sunken U-boat by the sound of knocking. We reported its bearings to the flagship and they were at once sent out to all ships taking part in the exercise, which then formed a circle round the area. She lay at a depth of 50 fathoms. The knocking showed that everybody had taken refuge in the two watertight compartments aft and that the for'ard section had been sealed off.

Fifty fathoms is a damnable depth. We knew that it is only possible to save entombed crews at lesser depths than this. I know myself a case when only three men out of sixty contrived to extricate themselves at 50 fathoms. The human body is simply not equal to the strain of the reduction in pressure when coming up to the surface from any considerable depth. It would take a day at least to bring a lighter from Kiel, and to send divers down with grappling gear would mean a waste of more valuable time, when the air in the two compartments aft could only last out fourteen hours for so many men; the engines in the sunken boat were not working and its air-purifying plant was out of order. In view of all this the flag officer decided to give orders for the men to come up. Every man had an escape-suit and there was a pressure chamber in the depot-ship to enable the men who came up too quickly to benefit from the gradual pressure-adjustment.

Incredibly high-pitched, but still just perceptible to the human ear, an underwater signal was sent out to them.

Flood up. Abandon ship. Surface illuminated by star-shell. Good luck. Flotilla Commander.

"Flood up. Abandon ship..." repeated the hydrophone operator quietly. How different from the way that Luftwaffe crews bale out! That contrast was in every mind. Of course, it is no fun to do a parachute jump, but you can't compare that with the physical and psychological strain of a submarine crew even in relatively shallow waters. Good luck, boys, we thought it could happen to any of us. For all the hopelessness of their plight we kept our thumbs up. The junior watch-keeper down there was a great friend of mine – be had been married six weeks.

We could hear the sound of water pouring in, through our hydrophone. Our comrades must be equalising the pressure without which the escape-hatch can't be opened. On every square centimetre there is 1-kilogram water pressure at a depth of 50 fathoms. That means 10 kilograms at 50 fathoms, and represents a 38-ton pressure on the whole deck. The hatchway itself is 70 centimetres in diameter. Flares were going up all the time, while hundreds of eyes scanned the surface. Many of us had friends in the sunken boat whose lives were now at stake. But still nothing emerged, no bubbles, not a sign of life. We waited for four hours in vain without even a knock. Perhaps they'd fainted and couldn't open the hatchway or the man first up was caught up in his gear and was blocking the passage for the rest.

After six hours had elapsed the exercise was resumed. You can't bring dead men to life – that's just the mercilessness of war. "Go in and sink', – sometimes it is the enemy, sometimes ourselves. While we are still high-spirited and confident we retain the will to live, even if tragedy is all about us. Dare anyone pass judgment? The death of our friends had made us only the more conscious of our own predicament.

CHAPTER FIVE

CHRISTMAS EVE

FOR four weeks the wind had been howling from every quarter at 55 to 60 miles an hour, with heavy rain and the thermometer only a few degrees above zero. I was up on the bridge. There was of course no protection there, just the icy steel bulkheads, so it was impossible to work up any warmth. Lashed to the rail as I was, the leather safety-belt reinforced with steel bit deep into my ribs. It had been known for the watch on the bridge to be washed overboard in heavy seas – in one boat the relief had gone up to take over and just found no one there. The force of the seas breaking over us now was terrific, but the boat shot on nevertheless like an arrow, with very little pitching or rolling and the waves going over us as over a breakwater.

The officer of the watch, who was standing for'ard with one rating, had warned the look-out aft of a big wave ahead. Ducking, we groped for something to hold on to and waited for it. It was indescribable. Everything went green as tons of sea-water poured over us, ears, nostrils and mouths choked and eyes blinded and stinging. Waterproof clothing, sea-boots and jackets weren't much use, for in spite of tying up every opening the ice-cold water still soaked in. My hands were stiff with cold, but I still had to keep my binoculars before my eyes, since it was a point of honour to let nothing escape us – we simply had to keep keyed up on the look-out for a sign of ship or plane.

The minutes before I was relieved ticked by unbelievably slowly. Half an hour to go, a quarter of an hour. In five minutes the first relief should be up. But still he didn't come.

Until the first man relieved came below the second relief was not allowed up. Only on very exceptional occasions was even one man, other than the duty watch, permitted on deck, for that would only have prolonged the time for getting every hand below when we had to dive in an emergency. Besides, it might also have distracted the attention of both watches while the relief was taking over. And of course we always had a surprise attack whenever our thoughts wandered for a moment, but when we were alert nothing ever did happen.

Relieved at last, and frozen to the marrow, I climbed below into the cold damp boat. Moisture trickled down the bulkheads. If only we could have switched the heating on, but that was against orders as we had to save current; electricity stored is as good a fuel as oil. As you use it up, so your radius of action shrinks, We just had to put up with it all – chattering teeth and everything. However, we knew the next action would warm us up and be much more effective than any heating system.

Of course a drop of Schnapps wouldn't have been a bad idea, but that wasn't allowed either, as it can slow up one's reflexes at times when every second counts. In one second we could cover 10 yards under water and it could make quite a difference whether a bomb hit aft or fell 10 yards astern. The engine-room staff had to react like lightning, and so had the duty-watch, particularly the officer of the watch. Swift obedience to orders makes a good U-boat crew. You don't often get time to think things over. You can give the right order automatically if you've got perfect self-discipline, but hesitation, nerves or any form of loss of self control are as likely as not to prove one's own death-sentence.

My fingers had gone stiff with the cold and I had to be helped out of my sodden clothes in order to change – not that we had all that amount of clothing aboard, as the lockers wouldn't hold it. We could either let our things dry on our bodies, or again put on the damp uniform we had worn on our last but one watch, for in eight hours in that humid atmosphere our clothes simply wouldn't dry. Nor could they be strung on a line just anywhere on board, either, as they might only too easily foul the diving levers and perhaps jam in them. Of course, our sea-boots were clammy with salt water inside and out and our leather outfits only dried out when the sun was shining and we didn't need them. A salty crust covered our clothes like hoar-frost.

So our hands would get to work mechanically on the damp change of clothing laid out for us, as we might at any moment have to jump to action stations. This would be followed by a gulp of hot tea, sausage, and rancid butter on a chunk of bread – remembering to cut the mould off first – and save what was over for bread-soup later on. We didn't really have to be quite so economical, still it was just conceivable that circumstances might crop up when we would have to last out on very little for a long time. I knew of a case when a U-boat, all its engines put out of action by depth-charges, returned to base four months overdue, by sail. The ship's company were down to eating their very shoe-leather.

So we turned in, fully-dressed save for our leather jackets and our boots, a great green stinking fur coat between ourselves and the icy bulkheads. So far I hadn't contracted rheumatism, and in fact I wasn't due for it till we had finished three more operations, if our general experience meant anything. But there were more immediate concerns than that: El Alamein and the Morocco and Algeria landings had reversed the outlook for us, while the position at Stalingrad was ominous. If our country was fighting for survival, what did the individual's troubles matter?

"Next watch stand by with oilskins. Gale still blowing from the north-west with heavy rain. Put on all the warmest clothes you've got."

So, at twenty minutes' notice, the next watch would go up for the familiar four hours' ordeal in the interminable wild weather of an Atlantic winter. We often kept watch in pairs in escape-gear, securing the hatch behind so that only the speaking-tube linked us with the world below. But don't imagine that an escape-suit is water-proof; it certainly should be at the top where it's sewn together, but in fact the water invariably seeps through and at the bottom the stuff's so thick that it can't run out. It just climbed higher and higher up our legs, and sometimes actually up to our navels. We would bore little holes in the soles of our shoes, which made things a bit better, but on these watches we grew thoroughly embittered, cursing the war and the world and the man who had invented submarines and everything else, including ourselves. And still the storm would go raging on.

At the end of 1940 we probably had only one submarine in the whole Atlantic. By 1941 we had twenty, and now, at Christmas 1942, we had many, many more. And yet what a contrast there was between all the successes those few U-boats had scored in the early days and the few all our submarines put together could achieve now! Why was it? The answer, of course, was Radar... U-boat warfare was revolutionised when the enemy discovered and exploited a principle already known to German science, and equipped his anti-U-boat forces with these extremely efficient detection sets. Radar is short for the English "Radio Detection and

Ranging" apparatus. In a few words, the gear consists of a very short-wave transmitter whose beam is reflected as if by a mirror when it meets a solid object. When the returning ray is picked up by a receiver, the time-difference is used to calculate the object's range. At the same time the direction can be established from the position of the transmitting aerial at the moment of reflection. British submarine chasers and planes no longer had to depend on their look-outs, for they could spot us now whenever we surfaced and in all weathers, in rain or fog or even in complete darkness, so that while our chances to attack grew less, our losses also grew heavier. Possibly the U-boat Command at first underestimated the potentialities of Radar but luckily at the eleventh hour, after our first series of setbacks, they began fitting us out with a counter-device which should at any rate give us warning of the enemy's presence and of any attempt he might be making to detect ours. This was an aerial in a square frame on the conning-tower made fast to the rail on a wooden pole and connected with our hydrophone by a thick rubber cable. We called the thing FuMB (*Funkmessbeobachter* – Radar search receiver).

But this gear was still rudimentary, one great drawback of it being that the 40-centimetres by 50-centimetres frame had to be hauled in at each alarm lest we should lose it altogether or, worse still, get it tangled in the cable that shut the hatch on the conning-tower.

It was Christmas Eve 1942. We thought perhaps we should cruise for a few hours dived this evening and play gramophone records. There will be something special for supper too – strawberries and whipped cream. We were specially fond of this dish and made a point of having it served up on special occasions. As a surprise the engine-room rigged us up a Christmas-tree with branches and pine needles of wood and coloured paper, cotton wool for snow and little pocket-torch bulbs in white sheathes which did well for candles. I was on watch from eight to twelve morning and night, in other words the "forenoon" and "first" watches. While I was keeping the "first" I got to thinking how the lights would be shining on our Christmas-tree at home and my family gathered round the presents with Father Christmas and the pictures of saints which I had loved as a child all decorated. But I had to put all that out of my mind – the thought of it was too distracting... round me it was pitch dark and great waves were breaking over the conning-tower. All of us up here were wet to the skin, and there were still two hours to go before we were relieved. We had left our binoculars in the conning-tower where they would be to hand and dry should anything suspect show up.

Suddenly something loomed ahead – but then things were always looming, every wave for us was an "object ahead". At my warning cry the boatswain's mate peered in the same direction.

"My glasses!"

"Object ahead!" the chap next to me confirmed. "Getting larger!"

Now I could make it out clearly with my glasses – an American destroyer. Crash dive! Ripping our steel safety-belts off we hurtled instinctively down the hatchway. In my haste I knocked over the FuMB aerial, not caring if it smashed.

The destroyer was nearly on top of us and must have sighted us... thank heaven for the heavy seas which would make accurate fire impossible. "Flood!" The order was given even though I was still up on deck – we had got used to doing it that way, in spite of it being laid down that the order should not be given until the hatch was shut. But every second counted now, the water was pouring into our tanks with the destroyer only a thousand yards away. I hung onto the hatch, but nothing would make it shut, and the sea was actually beginning to pour in. Salt smarted in my eyes as I struggled to find out what had gone wrong.

"Shut the vents! Blow tanks! Hatch jammed!"

My head was in a whirl. Was our number up on this of all nights? Why *wouldn't* the bloody thing work? At any moment the destroyer might ram us – it didn't just *happen* to be there, obviously they had picked us up with their Radar.

At last I got free of the hatch and was back on the bridge once again, the Commander with me. Neither of us spoke as we made frantic efforts to find out why the hatch had jammed. It wasn't long before we found the FuMB cable had got caught in it, though the aerial itself was below.

The destroyer was lying right across our bows now. We were so ridiculously close that we could not only see someone smoking on her bridge but practically make out the sound of Christmas celebrations.

With the enemy so clearly off their guard we gave up trying to dive. Our fate should have been in their hands, but now theirs seemed rather to lie in ours . . . we prepared for a surface attack.

"Tube number one ready-fire!"

Firing like this into raging seas was a hazardous affair, as with this terrific swell it was quite on the cards that the destroyer might be on the crest of a wave and the torpedo pass through the depths beneath. We waited impatiently. Perhaps the magnetic pistol wouldn't fire, or the tinfish had in fact missed its mark. The time for hitting had certainly long gone by. Yes – we had missed.

"Tube number two ready-fire!"

The range was 400 yards; we could get no closer, for 100 yards was the danger limit. If we had gone much nearer, with all the explosive we had on board we should have been in danger from the shock-wave of our own torpedo. Many U-boats were in fact lost this way.

Suddenly there was a flash of red, blue, yellow, green, and an enormous waterspout came tumbling down. In a minute or two the dark shadow ahead had disappeared. More than that, there wasn't a lifeboat, not a raft, not a sign of life of any kind. Sunk without trace as she was, it was pointless to look for survivors.

It had been evens whether we or the enemy were going to go to the bottom, and fate had decided to send them there. However, that was how we did in fact spend our Christmas 1942.

We still cruised on for some time patrolling our allotted area without anything turning up, but our fuel was falling to danger level. Then, just as we were looking forward to returning to harbour, and conjuring up visions of the depot-ship, our hopes were dashed when the wireless operator reported that there was a message for us in cypher. There are three kinds of such wireless messages – Code, which is the normal one; Cypher; and Commander's Cypher. Generally speaking, coded messages are decoded in the coding machine and reported and logged in plain language. The log has to be signed by the Commander every two hours. If a cypher comes in, the first word which comes out of the machine is "cypher", and the remainder cannot be decoded. To do this, a special setting of the machine is required, which is held only by the Commander and the Signal Officer. If, however, the next word of the text comes out as "Commander", he must himself carry on decoding, using yet another setting which is held by him alone.

This signal came from the U-boat Command, giving us course, speed and the rest of it, and adding *Important tankers. Attack*.

The Commander talked it over with the officers. We were very low in fuel, in fact with only just enough to make harbour and certainly none to spare for attacking tankers. But when we sent a signal to the C-in-C U-boats intimating this, the answer came in twenty minutes: Attack and sink. I never abandon a U-boat. Dönitz.

So we had had it. They would probably send out a refuelling boat, which would mean eight weeks more at sea in this filthy weather, which didn't show any sign of getting better. Our rubber clothing was practically in shreds with the wear-and-tear of constant alerts. "We'll peg out with rheumatism," we told each other, "they won't have to waste bombs on us." You can't stop grumbling, and we believed in saying what we thought. It was just a bloody awful sweat. Admiral Dönitz knew very well that our remarks were unprintable sometimes, but there was no way out of it.

After we had obtained bearings from other U-boats already in contact with the convoy, it eventually came into view and we attacked. I got one of the largest ships in the crosswires, my hand on the firing-push. There was a spurt of flame followed by a terrific explosion and we were flung against each other on the bridge.

I got two more ships focused in the crosswires.

Fire! Fire!

It was a matter of seconds. Guns were being fired by the escort. "Strange," remarked the Commander, but then we saw the reason for it – suddenly it grew as light as day as star-shell lit up the sky. Two ships were burning and more explosions were coming from where other U-boats had hit their targets. Crash dive! We had been sighted, and no wonder at that close range and in that fantastically brilliant light. A multiple pom-pom opened up on us. Red, green, yellow and blue tracer bullets went whizzing round the conning-tower, we were hit on the superstructure, threw ourselves flat and then dived down the hatchway. The enemy, thank heaven, were firing too high. We trimmed off at 125 fathoms. An ammunition ship had blown up when we were only 500 yards away and then came the depth charges, but we were used to that, and this time they only lasted six hours. There followed the order to surface and contact the convoy once more, but we couldn't make it, not with the best will in the world, with 4 tons of fuel left. If the supply-boat didn't turn up we would have to hoist our sails.

A ship was sighted, apparently a large one, but our hands were tied. A few hours at full speed and our fuel-tanks would be empty. Still, we sent out a signal, in the hope that another U-boat would find her.

CHAPTER SIX

UNDERWATER FUELLING

RIGHT from the start the refuelling of our U-boats had been a problem, and the longer the cruise the greater that problem was. To make this clear let me give the following data. The normal operational type of U-boat could cover 7,000 miles on each operational cruise, and it is 2,000 miles from a German North Sea port to mid-Atlantic, making the journey out and back 4,000 miles. That left 8,000 miles to be covered in actual operations. Moreover, we had to reckon that we couldn't take the shortest route because mines and other obstacles barred the way and involved détours.

As it was pointless to try to carry out operations in the waters round Great Britain, which could so easily be patrolled by planes and MTBs, it seemed far the better course to distribute our ships across the North Atlantic into still remoter waters like the Caribbean and the south Atlantic and so make the enemy spread his forces. In this, one of the chief tasks of the Naval Command, the distances involved caused great difficulty. From Hamburg it is 5,000 miles to New Orleans and 5,500 to Rio de Janeiro, which meant that the normal U-boat could not carry out this duty in spite of being easily mass-produced and having the best fighting qualities. Accordingly, although French bases like Bordeaux, Lorient, St Nazaire and Brest did not make the distances very much shorter, their value could not be overestimated in view of the fact that all German ports, indeed the whole North Sea, can easily be blockaded by minefields, nets and other contraptions. In World War One that became very obvious, for we suffered serious losses in our efforts to reach the Atlantic. In fact one may say that it is impossible to wage U-boat warfare successfully without Atlantic bases.

As soon as the Naval Command appreciated that it was essential to carry the war into distant waters the supply problem cropped up. At the beginning of the war, when we decided to station supply-ships at fixed points, we used converted merchantmen; but as far back as 1940 our losses were so high that this idea was soon abandoned in favour of another solution, the submarine tanker. These boats had a displacement of 2,000 tons and could supply ten U-boats with stores and fuel. Fruit, fresh vegetables and meat were kept in big refrigerators and there was even a bakery on board. Ten of these vessels, which also carried spare torpedoes, and looked to a non-specialist exactly like surface warships, were projected, and by 1942 there were several in service. These supply-boats increased the potential of the U-boats enormously, or, more precisely, of the type of U-boat that we were using. The construction of larger U-boats had to be abandoned because of the time involved in putting them into mass production.

Let us imagine that the U-boat Command sends ten U-boats to the coast of Central America. They can remain at sea for a total of three months. Two months are lost on passage out and home, leaving one month only for actual operational service. If, therefore, ten boats are required in the area for three months, thirty boats in all are necessary. Against this, ten boats, if supplied by one supply-boat, can stay up to four months in the area. From these figures it is clear that the provision of one supply-boat to every ten operational boats can more than treble the time that the latter are able to spend on operations.

In order to avoid misunderstanding it should be emphasised that when several boats were together in one area, they operated basically as single units, and the term "pack-tactics" is usually wrong when used in this particular connection. The obligation to help one another to find convoys did not mean subordination to any kind of "pack" leadership. The U-boat Commanders received their orders without exception direct from the High Command – Admiral Dönitz.

He confined himself to indicating positions and taking general charge of the campaign. Apart from this, Commanders could always change their area of operations if they considered it desirable, on grounds of too strong escorts, changes of convoy-routes, etc. The command of a U-boat was undoubtedly one of the most independent jobs in the whole war, perhaps more so than that of a commanding General.

Now look at it from the enemy's point of view. Suddenly U-boats appeared in remote waters. He had to draw destroyers and U-boat chasers away from the vital North Atlantic, and then to assemble convoys, with all the delays which that involves. Harbours could only cope with a limited number of ships at a time: the rest were forced to wait till moles, berths and cranes were available, and once loaded every ship had similarly to wait till the last was ready to put to sea. At sea again the fastest craft had to adjust its speed to the slowest, while the need to zigzag considerably lengthened each voyage. Finally, when the convoys reached their destination, the whole process had to be gone through all over again at the other end. The advantages to us were thus threefold – a weakening of the enemy's forces in the North Atlantic, a general slowing-up of his supply system, and of course a reduction of his available shipping-space through our successful attacks.

We had plenty of time to think about all this while we were trying to find our supply-boat. When at last, the storm having abated a little, we made wireless contact, it was high time, as we had only a ton of fuel left. For many days we had been unable to take star-sights as the sky was clouded over and rain fell incessantly. Our hopes that we would find her were countered by the reflection that the Atlantic was very big and that we were very small... yet it would be fatal if we missed her. Eventually, our fuel running out, we decided to cut off our engines and make homing-signals; and so every two hours they went out over the ether.

But at last our problems were resolved – we sighted the supply-boat. A piece of our own country, a partner in our fate – what a moment it was! But still we were concerned that the heavy seas might upset our plans, for it was impossible to stand on deck for fear the waves would wash us overboard. We knew that if the enemy came on us in this critical plight we were lost. The whole day we waited in vain. After nightfall we could still vaguely sense the position of the other boat, but we dared not go close in for fear of ramming. One dark object looks much like another by sea at night, and this night was black as pitch and the waves mountain-high.

Light broke at last and the wind seemed to be dropping, although the sea was still lashing at the deck. The chief engineer and some of the engine-room staff went for'ard and aft to open the fuelling valves and clear the way for the supply-hose. Icy cold though it was, these men wore only bathing trunks, the belt to which they were lashed biting into their flesh. At times one or other of them would even be washed overboard and only be hauled in again with a good deal of effort. It wasn't exactly fun for them but it was the only way.

We were cruising parallel to the supply-boat, perhaps 90 yards away. A line was fired over us by pistol, and this was followed by the hose and a towing-wire. We breathed again as the precious fluid began to flow in. Altogether we took in 20 tons of it, not to speak of bread, potatoes, vegetables and other food in watertight sacks. The whole thing went off perfectly, although it was our first experience.

Another U-boat called up, wanting to be victualled too. Short of a certain quantity of oil, we had taken all we needed aboard, but for security reasons and also to test our manoeuvrability under water we both dived; first the supply-boat, then ourselves. The two boats proceeded one astern of the other with lines, hose and wire left in place, and so we cruised for three hours on end at a depth of 95 fathoms. It was a fantastic conception; we were embarking Diesel oil under water for the first time in history. Keeping in contact with our hydrophones we continued to indicate our course and speed, until our tanks were filled and we could surface. To top up, we took aboard a few extras, lobsters and other delicacies – we had had enough of tinned foods. The next thing was to get as far away as possible as quickly as we could. In no circumstances must the supply-boat be discovered, as its loss would be a serious setback in our U-boat war. Of course the prolonged operational cruise that all this made possible didn't exactly suit the men, who would have been quite content to go home after three months at sea. But effective tactics aren't so easy to reconcile with human feelings.

CHAPTER SEVEN

GIBRALTAR WAS HELL

A CLOUD of smoke was reported ahead and we made for it at full speed. Then suddenly it vanished, though the sound of propellers could still be heard in the same direction. For at least an hour we maintained our course, and then listened in again. Now the sound came from exactly the opposite direction. It was all very odd, for we could see quite clearly, and in any case no ship could possibly have moved over to the other beam as fast as that. At last we saw the "smoke cloud" – a whale spouting! We didn't let the watch on the bridge forget that one for a very long time.

Fog came down, and with it again the sound of propellers made itself heard. We headed towards it but nothing was to be seen. You hear best at great depths and we went to 95 fathoms. The hydrophone-operator reported "80 revolutions, something approaching. Now there's something else, Diesel engines I think." He suddenly gave a yell and tore off his earphones and clapped his hands to his ears. We had all heard the explosion, though not of course so loud as the unfortunate chap at the hydrophone. Listening in again: "Only Diesels audible, quieter," he told us. It was bad luck, but we had been beaten to it. The first sound was a steamer, the second a torpedo exploding, the third a U-boat. We had many such experiences on our cruise, but we didn't mind – they were nothing compared with the pleasant prospect of stretching our legs ashore once again.

St Nazaire. It was the first time we had berthed in a U-boat pen. It was a triumph of technique, twelve bunkers each large enough to take three U-boats, separated by ferro-concrete three feet thick, and which could be completely shut off by lowering huge steel shutters. The docks and repair-shops were marvellously protected, for the roofing was over 20 feet thick, and no bomb could pierce that – the few that fell had no serious effect, and work went on without a break under the heaviest air attack. There were no more hold-ups in U-boat production now. The figures were impressive. Some half a million tons of ferro-concrete were being turned out for the work at a cost of a hundred and twenty-five million marks – pens going up all along the French coast, notably at Lorient.

When we went on leave our Flotilla Commander sat next to me in the train, and he told me how our U-boat service was developing.

"There's no more room in the pens," he said. "We just don't know where to berth the boats when they put in, so they are going to have to extend the whole system of bunkers. Do you realise that a U-boat puts to see every other day, and a short time ago we had three hundred in the North Atlantic all at once? Just think of it!"

Indeed, I knew that our successes in the last few months had been more numerous than at any time in the war.

In Berlin I joined my family and also found my brother at home, who was stationed in Norway and always managed to make his leave coincide with mine. He was six years my senior, having been born in the First World War. In those days my father had been on active service, but now my mother had to bear the greater hardship of agonisingly long stretches without news from her son at sea. What is more, the war didn't seen to be going well and air raids were being stepped up. Although our propaganda was adept at turning out impressive arguments and public morale was amazingly good, there was some heart-searching in certain circles. Personally, I couldn't help anxiously reflecting on American production, for in 1938 I had seen the Ford works turn out five thousand cars a day. The key to victory clearly lay in our capacity to stop material from the USA reaching other fronts. But were our U-boats up to it? We who were on active service did not know the answer – how could we? We had no idea of Germany's industrial potential, nor how far new U-boats' developments had gone. But one thing we did know and had to face – we could not go on waging submarine warfare as we had been doing. The latest reports of tonnage sunk didn't blind us to the fact that the enemy was making our work harder every day, nor to the truth that our own losses were mounting terribly. Radar, especially aircraft radar, was turning out to be the enemy's trump card. Admiral Dönitz's latest order of the day was "Don't let aeroplanes worry you. Just shoot them down." And indeed all the fronts combined had so pinned down the Luftwaffe that they had lost command of the Bay of Biscay which we had to cross every time we went to sea and returned to harbour. Areas where, two years previous, we hardly ever saw an enemy plane were now controlled by them, and we found ourselves obliged to dive every two hours as a defence-measure.

Meanwhile we had been fitted with a four-barrel "Vierling" AA-gun which was mounted on a platform abaft the conning-tower, while four of the latest type machine-guns completed our armament. To test a U-boat's defensive power against air attack two specially equipped AA-boats had been fitted out with armour-plated conning-towers and equipped with light AA and heavy machine-guns, the idea being to lure aircraft to attack under the impression that these were ordinary type U-boats, and then to open up with a surprise salvo. We seemed certain of success, and our Command hoped that this would deter the enemy's airmen from attacking us in future. In fact it worked out rather differently.

On one occasion, for instance, one of these AA-boats surfaced in the Bay of Biscay, and shortly afterwards two planes appeared and the action started. It soon transpired that the planes had 4-centimetre guns while our AA-boat only carried guns of the 2-centimetre type. The planes kept out of range and from a safe distance wiped out everyone on deck before the submarine could dive. It was hopeless from the start. Fourteen were killed, two of them officers, and the Commander badly wounded. Taking the only way out, they dived after all, and the boat was amazingly lucky to reach harbour. This was a highly discouraging episode for us all. Still Dönitz would not change his mind. New types of U-boat were being planned and the search for defensive devices was unremitting. I suppose he could not alter his strategy overnight. All one can say is that he never spared either himself or those who served under him – both his sons had died as U-boat officers.

So once again we put out into the Atlantic. Twice we dived to attack but had to break off action as the steamers turned out to be neutrals – too absurd! For a long time after we sighted nothing, but the whole time we were gradually nearing the straits of Gibraltar, through which so much enemy shipping must inevitably pass.

It was a fine spring day without a cloud in the sky, and we could clearly see the Rock, that British fortress commanding the Mediterranean. So here were the pillars of Hercules, the Jebel Tarik, fresh from playing one more fateful role in history. Under its protection the invasion fleet had mustered and the African landings been carried out – since when the African campaign was drawing to its end and they were preparing to invade Italy.

Finally, the culmination of our monotonous waiting, we sighted great plumes of smoke and innumerable mastheads. But almost immediately planes appeared and we were obliged to dive. Had they spotted us? If so, warships would be on our trail within an hour. It was a fine day, but not too good for us, for the sea was glassily calm, perfect for their Asdic. A report came from the hydrophone operator:

"Propellers at high speed. Probably destroyers. Trying to pick us up on their Asdics."[1]

"Dive to 75 fathoms. Silent speed."

We were all ready, with our felt shoes on and all but the most essential lighting shut off to save current, as we had no idea how long the hunt would last. The enemy were in triangular formation, with us in the middle, and I must say they worked superbly. We had never known the first charges to fall with such uncomfortable accuracy as these did, invariably six at a time. All the glass panels on our controls were shattered and the deck was strewn with splinters. Valve after valve loosened, and before long the water came trickling through. The attack went on unremittingly for three hours without a break, the charges falling thicker and thicker around us, cruising as we were now at a depth of 100 fathoms. With the need to save current we were working the hydroplane and steering-gear by hand, and meanwhile the hydrophone was picking up more destroyers, though only the men within earshot knew it. What was the point of upsetting the others?

Faces are pale, and every foreheads sweating. We all know what the other man's thinking. There are six destroyers now, three of them heading for Gibraltar, but fresh ones always coming up in relay. Like this they'll never run out of depth-charges – our position's truly desperate, the fine weather dead against us. Why doesn't a storm blow up, like it always did when we were on our way here?

By the time we have had sixteen hours of it we have long given up counting the depth-charges. During this time no one's had any sleep, and we've all dark rings under our eyes. Plenty of bulbs have broken, but we don't change them – with the emergency lighting we can only guess the position of the various installations. The darkness makes it all the more frightening.

There've been tricky moments before, but this time it's just hell. At times we have to dive to 126 fathoms. The steel bulkhead supports are

[1] English equipment for underwater search is call "Asdic" derived from the "Anti-Submarine Detector Indicator Committee" which developed it.

buckling and may give at any moment. But perhaps just because of this we're calm.

"Well, it's not everyone who gets such an expensive coffin," a dry voice remarks. "Four million marks it cost."

Yes, when it happens it'll be quick enough.

If only we could defend ourselves, see something to shoot at – the sense of being trapped into inactivity is unbearable. The current is down to danger level, the compressed air cylinders almost empty and the air itself tastes leaden. Our oxygen is scarce, our carbon monoxide content continually increasing, so that we're breathing with difficulty like so many marathon runners in the last mile; at this rate we can last out twenty hours longer and then we'll just have to surface. We know what will happen then, we've read the dispatches: as soon as the U-boat surfaces, all the warships open fire, and the bombardment goes on even though the crew have begun to jump overboard – they must be made to lose their nerve and forget to sink their boat. It was one of the enemy's dearest wishes to capture a U-boat, as that would have made it so much easier to devise means of countering the German underwater threat.

"Stand by for depth charge attack!" They are falling right alongside now. A roar and a crash in the control-room enough to crack our eardrums – fragments of iron fly around – valves smash to bits. in spite of oneself one can't help stretching a hand out towards one's escape-gear. The petty officer in the control-room has his hand on the flood valve to let in compressed air for surfacing, but he's still awaiting the Commander's orders, and all the time they are still thundering at us. The helmsman shouts that the compass has been blown out of its frame with its 10,000 revolutions a minute the gyro wheel goes spinning round the boat, but luckily none of us is hit.

In a council of war with the officers, the Commander admitted the situation was pretty hopeless; it might even be that we should have to surface and sink the boat. On the other hand the moon would not rise until two in the morning and it would be dark till then – if we surfaced in the dark, there was still just a hundred-to-one chance we might break out of the trap that way. Meanwhile everything was ready to blow up the boat. Time fuses were laid against the torpedo warheads and in other vulnerable places all over the ship so that if one didn't explode there was every chance that another would. In no circumstances must we fall into enemy hands and as a result be responsible for the deaths of many fellow U-boat men. Next we distributed escape-gear and lifeboats – a one-man collapsible rubber dinghy per head. The Commander and bridge watch put on red glasses to accustom their eyes to the dark so that they should be able to see the moment that we surfaced – I couldn't help thinking this superfluous, for inside the boat it was as good as pitch dark anyhow. Next the Asdic decoys were thrown out, and we began to fill balloons with metal strips attached which were to be released when we surfaced to float low over the water and fox the enemy radar.

As we prepared to surface at 50 fathoms we caught the sound of Asdics even more distinctly. Damn it, they'd still got us! As we shot up to 25 fathoms we could hear loud explosions. The hydrophone operator announced:

"Destroyers at close quarters. Six different propellers turning.

Swearing, the Commander gave the order to surface. By now we couldn't make full speed as the batteries weren't up to it. We brought up ammunition for the AA-guns, large magazines with fifty rounds in each. Five torpedo-tubes could fire simultaneously, and so could four machine-guns. The belts of these latter did not give out like they do on machine guns ashore, but, stretching right down the conning-tower into the control-room, were constantly replenished so as to fire between them 6,400 rounds a minute. We could turn them on like hoses. Up to 2,000 metres we could menace a destroyer and outside 2,000 metres the destroyer couldn't spot us. Yet we knew that if it did come to an engagement we should certainly get the worst of it. We just hoped that we would not have to open fire and might get away unnoticed.

We drove to the surface as depth charges were still dropping around us. The Asdic decoys were obviously fulfiling their purpose. All of a sudden the conning-tower hatch burst open and we almost shot out of it. The pressure was terrific. The Commander looked out to port and I to starboard. Thank heaven it was a dark night and the sky was overcast. We made out three destroyers, one 100 metres away at most, still dropping depth charges. We started up both Diesel engines and rang down full speed at once – no time to let them warm up. The generators were going too, as we had to recharge our batteries, besides the two compressors recharging the compressed-air cylinders. The fans began to drive fresh air through the boat. The fresh air tore into our lungs: we could hardly stand up and were practically fainting. Guns and machine-guns were loaded and trained on the nearest destroyer, but we all hoped it wouldn't sight us for both our sakes. We had a new type of torpedo that could zig-zag or make circular tracks, but we weren't starting anything. Had we done so we couldn't have got away unmolested, since we lacked a good supply of two essentials; current and compressed air. The range started to increase and the ten gas-filled balloons we had released went up and drifted with the wind. The enemy radar would be amazed to pick up so many U-boats all at once. He presumably suspected the presence of still more where the Asdic decoys were in action. We could well imagine the sort of activity going on just then on the bridge of one of these destroyers: Radar operator: "Ship bearing 040 degrees, range 6,000 metres. Fifteen more echoes on various bearings." Destroyer Captain: "Plot the position of the hunting group and put on the chart." Navigator: "Instructions carried out." Captain. "Course so-and-so. Report radar bearings continuously." The destroyer approaches its target (a balloon). Searchlights are sweeping. The Radar echo fades out and the range is now under 1,000 metres, the minimum range of the Radar sets of that time. Guns swing round – nothing to be seen, for the wires hanging from the balloons are very thin. Radar operator: "Echo right astern, probably the same object." Captain: "B–! We've overshot. Keep a better look out there! These damned U-boats are too small. Might well slip a fish into us into the bargain. Hard a-starboard!"

At last we lost sight of the destroyers. The enemy Radar was confused by all the echoes, and even if the destroyers did pick us out in the dark they could not go all out after us for fear of ramming other British ships.

After an hour we had taken in fresh air enough to cruise underwater for sixteen hours, and in two hours we were all fit for duty again though terribly exhausted. We dived to 50 fathoms and left Gibraltar as far away and as fast as we could. I thought of the proverb, "When an ass steps on thin ice he generally falls through." Our ice had certainly been thin enough.

CHAPTER EIGHT

The Worst Enemy

IT IS impossible to tell the story of the U-boat war without discussing Radar, since it turned the tide of the battle of the Atlantic against us at the most critical stage of the war. For all the heroism and efficiency of our crews the power of the U-boat was shattered overnight. Let us get things clear. The word U-boat (*Unterseeboot*) gives a false impression. It should really be called a *Tauchboot* or Submersible, for until the beginning of 1943 we almost always cruised on the surface. You can see by its shape that a U-boat is built for surface work. The naked eye could scarcely ever distinguish it unless the crew made it conspicuous through their carelessness. By night it was invisible, by day it could always sight ships or planes before it was spotted because it was so small, a factor which enabled it to destroy the most powerful warships afloat. It could always dive before it was seen, moreover, and either attack dived or surface again after a prudent lapse of time and continue its operational programme. As it could stay dived for two days at a time it could cross the most strongly patrolled waters, or remain in them, because it could always surface at night to charge the batteries and change the air – generally a two-to four-hour job.

The U-boat's value in a surface engagement, however, was diminished by its extreme vulnerability; a faster surface ship equipped with guns and torpedo-tubes being more than a match for it. By the nature of its construction it could be sunk very easily. Furthermore, being constructed for diving underwater, a submarine on the surface has very little reserve buoyancy. A 500-ton surface craft, for example, can ship anything up to 500 tons of water before sinking, but a submarine of the same displacement only needs about a fifth of that amount. Surface craft, again, can usually find and repair a leak – not so a U-boat. All its complex fittings, engines, batteries and so forth get in the way the whole time.

When the war began the enemy realised that the Achilles heel of the U-boat service was its bases. The U-boat had to enter and leave harbour twice on each operational cruise, and the enemy knew where the bases were and would station his own boats outside them. Still, in the first years of the war our armament was up to his and the attempt to blockade us failed. Subsequently his plan to destroy the bases and repair-shops by air attack was thwarted by our timely construction of bunkers.

But Radar changed everything. The British scientists who saw and developed its possibilities were certainly not undeserving of the high honours which they were awarded. Germany knew the principle too. Our capital ships carried similar devices, though they were awkward and heavy, weighing up to 20 tons, while the Würzburg device was in regular use by our AA defences. But where the enemy stole a march on us was in his discovery of small and practicable instruments, especially the kind that could be fitted into aircraft. That was a step forward indeed. True, he could not locate us when dived, but the effect of Radar on our surface activities was more than disastrous, since it robbed us of our chief asset – invisibility in night attack.

The following is a rough description of the condition of Radar at the end of the war.

The sets used on active service were roughly the size of a radiogram, containing both transmitter and receiver, the Radar aerial, used both for transmission and for reception, being always placed at the highest part of the ship and in constant use. On a screen like that of a television-set the objects showed up in little dots of light, the direction of movement being indicated by the change of bearing, while the range was indicated on a separate scale. In this way the radio operator knew not only of the presence of all ships in his area, but also their range, bearing and approximate course.

Weather conditions were no obstacle, and warships equipped with Radar were in a position to open fire on any target at a considerable range even at night or in fog.

There is one important point that must not be overlooked: short waves do not travel round the curvature of the earth's surface, but in a straight line like rays of light. Everybody knows that you get a better view from a hilltop than you do on a plain. The same principle is also true of Radar – the greater its height the more effectively it works. Planes could thus use it more effectively than ships or shore establishments. On the other hand, Radar could not pick up an object underwater, which was naturally very important for us indeed. But its effect while we were surfaced – and we had to surface fairly often – was quite bad enough.

Now let us consider the overall position as it affected us. Newly-constructed boats from Germany, as also those stationed in Norway, had to pass between Britain and Iceland, while those based on France had to cross the Bay of Biscay. Now both these approaches were strictly patrolled by enemy planes and U-boat chasers, and our one alternative the English Channel – was too narrow and too shallow for us. Enemy Radar then could pick up a U-boat whenever it lay on the surface and we had to surface every day for three hours in order to charge our batteries. You can reckon that a plane equipped with Radar could at that time pick up a surfaced U-boat at 95 miles, in other words it was effective over a circle 190 miles in diameter, While a ship's Radar could pick us up at 20 miles, so that there was in effect no way we could get through to the Atlantic without being discovered.

Suppose, then, that we were to charge our batteries by night. A plane would pick us up with Radar, set its apparatus and follow our course with no trouble at all, always flying fore and aft of our boat so as to be able to make a direct run at us. We, on the other hand, would never know the plane was there, for you can't spot planes in the dark, and the noise of its engines would be drowned by our own. About 1,000 yards off it would switch on a powerful searchlight, pick out our stern and then drop its bombs, four or six of them. As the planes always dived to 150 feet before they dropped their bombs they invariably hit with deadly accuracy. The U-boat would have no time to bring its AA-guns to bear, and even if it had, the gun-crews would probably be dazzled by the sudden blaze of light, taken unawares and mown down. On such occasions it was a rare thing for any man on board to be saved.

The wisest thing was to surface by day. When the skies were clear and if our look-outs were alert we couldn't be surprised by planes. If the day was cloudy the conditions would be more or less the same as at night, but with this important difference – the plane had to adjust its altitude to the height of the clouds and was always in danger of being shot down when it emerged from the cloudbank. But, happen what might, they always did find us even if we got a chance to dive, since our range and bearing would be signalled at once to all ships, planes and shore establishments and in a few hours the area would be cordoned off. The U-boat would probably dive and might have enough electric power to proceed underwater. But for how long? Taking its cruising speed as nine knots, that meant it could travel nine miles an hour for twenty-four hours at most, enabling it to proceed underwater for a distance of 72 nautical miles, or in other words about 91 ordinary miles. After that a U-boat would be compelled to surface to recharge its batteries.

Now a circle of 91 miles radius could be effectively patrolled, with the result that the moment a U-boat surfaced the enemy Radar would pick it up even quicker than before, causing it to dive once more. Usually at this point the airmen would drop a buoy fitted with a homing device which emitted regular signals and acted as a beacon for the guidance of reinforcing ships and aircraft.

This much shorter time for charging batteries meant cutting down the time they could travel underwater on the electric motors. They thus had to surface more and more frequently till their batteries ran dry, after which the U-boat was an easy prey. The effect of all this was that we lost more and more U-boats, fewer and fewer returning to base, and those that went to sea seldom reaching the Atlantic at all.

At this stage Germany countered with FuMB, which some people loosely called counter-Radar. But in fact it was not a complete counter to Radar, for it only warned us when we had been picked up and so gave us time to dive before the enemy could follow up his discovery. Now Radar, as we have seen, both transmits and receives on very short waves. The receiving set is designed to make the reflected waves visible to the eye, the bearing being indicated by the direction in which the aerial is trained, and its range by the time that has elapsed between transmission and reception. As the waves travel round the earth about three times every second you can see how complex these devices must be to ensure accuracy. The FuMB is simply a Radar receiver, with the difference that it can be tuned to several different wave-lengths.

Imagine a man shouting at a wall. He is both transmitting with his mouth and receiving with his ears, an exact parallel to what we are describing. He picks up the reflected sound waves with his ears in the form of an echo. So let us call that man A and let him stand for Radar.

But now put another man, whom we will call B and who is dumb, against the wall. B will hear A's shout much more clearly than A will hear the echo of his own voice. B, of course, is FuMB. But now suppose that our wall moves steadily away from A, who is still shouting. A point will be reached when A can no longer hear the echo of his own voice. At this point, however, his shouts will still be clearly audible to B.

Thus a U-boat equipped with FuMB could always dive before an enemy attacked and you might thus think that our U-boats were again in a position to fulfil their original purpose. But you would be wrong, for what we could do underwater was a very small proportion of our total potential. Our most effective work was always done on the surface.

FuMB was much cheaper and simpler to operate than Radar, but it only enabled us to adopt a passive defence, and passive defence was no solution to our problem. The main difficulties with which Radar faced us could not be overcome by this means.

Meanwhile the fight between Radar and counter-Radar went a stage further. The Allies designed a receiver which could pick up the faint oscillations emitted by FuMB, which they used with their normal Radar sets switched off. So while we felt perfectly safe we were in fact betraying our bearings to the enemy by using our anti-Radar protection, and every time we used it we brought on our own destruction. In a single month of 1943 we lost thirty-five submarines in this way.

The High Command was in a quandary. Grand-Admiral Dönitz confirmed all U-boats to harbour and ordered those at sea to stop using their FuMB. That naturally left the enemy free to make effective use of his Radar again and our passage through the Bay of Biscay began to verge on the suicidal. Luckily my own boat got through. We were picked up one night, but our look-outs knew their jobs, were quick to spot approaching planes, dark though it was, and so gave us the time to use our AA-guns or, alternatively, to dive. That way we came back to base in safety.

CHAPTER NINE

Air Attack

AFTER our Gibraltar experience I went to Berlin on eight days' leave and the night I arrived the sirens went. For the first time I was actually able to use my gas-mask, not against gas but against the stifling smoke – an incendiary fell on our house, but we soon put it out. All the doors and windows were blown in, though, and as there was no available labour we had to do the repairs ourselves. That's how that leave was spent!

I returned to base to find that we were confined to harbour. Admiral Dönitz was inspecting our flotilla and gave us an address on the functions of the U-boat weapon, in the light of our lack of success. "If we stopped sending out U-boats," he said, "the enemy would stop escorting his convoys. As it is, we know that our U-boats are pinning down about two million enemy personnel in warships and in repair shops, quite apart from the time he loses through having to operate the convoy system at all. So we must keep our U-boats at sea even if they never sink a ship. Their mere presence alone constitutes a success for us."

Three days after leaving harbour again we got diphtheria aboard. Several of our men went down and we had an excuse to return to base – and, temporarily, to breathe freely once more. Recently we had been compelled to make our wills before we put to sea. So good for morale! The U-boat pens were empty, yet only three months before they had been planning to build new ones! The picture had certainly changed. As it was, we spent a pleasant time in the seaside resort of La Baule, near our base. We were all

The Type II, carried only five torpedos in total, therefore were used mainly for training.

Firing depth-charges.

A U-boat under air attack.

A U-boat crew awaiting rescue.

A U-boat crew survivor being helped on deck.

A battered U-boat's crew lining the deck before diving overboard.

Konrad Georg Heinz Schaeffer as Commander of his first Submarine U-148

The 'Grey Wolf'; Commander Schaeffer after a long journey

Depth-charges straddling a U-boat.

Survivors from a sunken U-boat.

A U-boat under fire from a Sunderland.

A U-boat refitted with additional anti-aircraft guns to act as a 'flak' or aircraft trap.

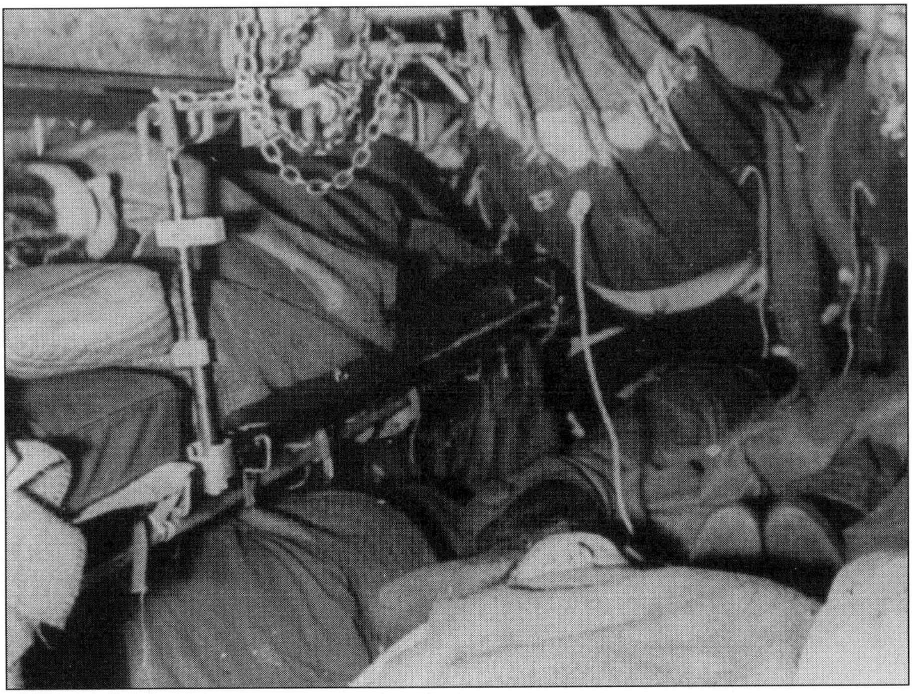

Bow torpedo room with sleeping crew, showing the cramped conditions under which the men lived.

Anyone entering an operational U-boat for the first time confused by the mass of stores covering essential machinery. Every available space was used.

U-977 is torpedoed in a test by USS Atule off Cape Cod, Massachusetts on November 13, 1945

in quarantine and lived in a house by the sea where we could sunbathe and get proper exercise. Nobody was in a hurry to go back to sea and no one ever suggested that we might soon be fit for duty. We just hung on the medical reports. It was advisable to leave well alone when it came to chance outbreaks of disease that kept us ashore. Another U-boat went out instead of us, but it didn't come back. Hardly any did now. We all knew that and had to reconcile ourselves to it. We always saw off the crews of outgoing U-boats and watched till they disappeared from sight. No more parties were given to celebrate the start of an operation now – we just drank a glass of champagne in silence and shook hands, trying not to look each other in the eyes. We had got pretty tough, but it shook us all the same. Operation Suicide! Many friends of mine had not come back. We had the same background and the same tastes, we were in the same service and had the same duties. Each of us had had his share of fighting in these long wartime years, though nobody made much of it. Heroics are for people who have never known what the real thing is.

At length we were passed fit, and our time was up. We had a special mission, our destination Freetown in West Africa. The conning-tower was rebuilt with a step aft which carried a "Vierling" quadruple AA-gun and two twin-mounted fully automatic 8-centimetre guns. Our machine-guns were replaced by newer models, and armour-plated shields reinforced the conning-tower, the purpose being to give the men self-confidence when attacked from the air. They afforded complete protection against machine-gun fire, but unfortunately aircraft have cannon too... The complement was increased to man all these AA-guns, and to complete the newcomers we took a doctor on board.

One night we were all sitting in the great glass winter garden of our hotel, bearded and bewhiskered. The French brandy was excellent and we did it full justice, for in four days we were due to sail. It was long past midnight and a storm was raging outside. I should explain here that we had a superstition that once a ship changed its complement it would fail to return from the next operation, so it was not surprising that experienced U-boat men as a whole were very against shifting personnel. In any case we no longer took officer cadets on active service to give them practical experience, since by now our losses were too high and manpower too scarce. In a word, the war had gone on too long. Anyway, while we were sitting there a doctor came up to our table. We knew who he was by his uniform because he was wearing the War-services Cross, issued for valuable service on the home front. We respected that enormously, in other words it was like a red rag to a bull.

"Are you from *U X*? I've been appointed to you–" and he introduced himself. The next moment he was going off into an explanation that he didn't really want to serve in U-boats and was in very poor health anyhow. Something to do with his ears. Besides, he wasn't really a surgeon but a gynaecologist, whereas our main requirement was ability to deal with wounds. Well, he had just done all he could, but apparently he couldn't get out of operational service. Grand chap, we thought to ourselves; we've certainly picked a winner.

"We're off in four days, you know," the chief engineer said briefly. "Bad times these. Written your will? No? Well, you must. Not many of us get back."

"Yes, so I understand," the doctor replied. "However, as we're confined to harbour for the present we don't need to worry. As I said, there's something wrong with my ears and I want them thoroughly examined."

"Sorry, but you've had it, old chap," said the second officer of the watch. "Home-port or not, we're off in four days, so you'd better send home your watch and wedding-ring, and don't forget to bid the folks at home goodbye. You know just how it is, what with thirty-five U-boats lost last month."

Our doctor was overwhelmed at this and really did send all his valuables home, miserably convinced he would never see his family again.

When our AA defence was strengthened a siren was fitted in addition to the alarm bell, specially designed to give warning of air attack. To choose the right button of siren or alarm bell (and the two were right next to each other), was a decision that involved life and death. Under what precise circumstances were we to ring the alarm bell and dive, or sound the siren and take up action stations at the AA-guns? That depended entirely on the position of the plane when we sighted it. Generally speaking, if it was more than 4,000 metres away – though of course much depended on the type of plane we were to avoid the risk of an encounter by diving, and then to ring the alarm bell. But if the plane was any closer it made no difference whether we dived or not as far as escaping its attentions was concerned, the point being that when a U-boat is in the process of diving the stern becomes a prominent target and the pilot has time to come down to drop his bombs without meeting any opposition. With a plane overhead we were only relatively safe at a depth of 26 fathoms. So when a plane was less than 4,000 metres away – in other words, sighted too late – we were to sound the siren and stand by our guns.

Admiral Dönitz thought we could hang on by two means till a non-radiating Radar search-receiver had been devised: first by giving us strong

AA defence and secondly by sending out U-boats in formations through the Bay of Biscay. He worked it out this way: if two planes find it all they can do to attack one U-boat, then three U-boats must be safe against six planes, and it is highly improbable that six planes will ever show up at the same time. Consequently several U-boats in company should be able to cross the Bay of Biscay in complete safety. Unfortunately he overlooked one rather important factor and we had to pay for it.

When our hour finally struck, we drank our farewell glass of champagne in traditional fashion. But this time when we slipped out into the Bay of Biscay there was no band to send us off.

We soon picked up the other two U-boats which had sailed from other bases to make up our experimental formation of three. The Commander of one of the other boats was the senior officer and so entitled to advise the remainder what to do, and hope that they would do it – for when it comes to the point every U-boat usually acts as it pleases. We fired all our guns every day, and the effect was most impressive, the automatic guns going off at an amazing rate. Each boat was able to fire eight barrels and a number of twin machine-guns. In a few days the test came with our being first of the three to sight a plane. Its range was 10,000 metres and so we had time to dive. We had agreed to wave a yellow flag for diving and a red one for defensive action – this time we waved our yellow one. But the other boats didn't see it. As the plane, a Sunderland, approached, we waved our red flag and opened fire on it but since the other boats happened to be busy with their daily target practice they failed to grasp what was happening. Luckily it was us the Sunderland decided to attack first. At 4,000 metres we opened fire. Little grey clouds started bursting round it and wisely it made off, only to change its mind and begin flying in circles round all three boats, at more than 4,000 metres and so just out of range of our guns. But, still we had no time to dive, though knowing exactly what would happen.

In ten minutes another plane showed up, as expected – a Liberator this time. It tried to attack the senior officers boat but was driven off. Individual planes could not harm us, we were too strong for them, so they kept on circling overhead at a safe distance. But soon more planes would show up, since we were near the coast of England, and probably destroyers too. The destroyers would approach to 5,000 yards and sink one boat after the other with their 15-centimetre guns. Conceivably some of the planes might join in for fun, but they would be quite superfluous, as with their superior armament the destroyers could easily do the job.

Both planes now circling overhead, we tried to keep our stern, where we had the greatest firepower, towards them, so we had to alter course and proceed at high speed in order to be as manoeuvrable as possible, with the inevitable result that we got separated. Still, we were close enough together for two boats to dive if the third protected them with covering fire, but that third U-boat would be doomed. The senior officer now signalled *Dive as opportunity arises*. We had hardly signalled back *Understood* when the stern of his boat began to rise out of the water, as he started to dive. Then I watched the Sunderland attack. When it came down to 30 feet we opened fire, and the plane increased its altitude, our shells meanwhile falling short, as we were too far away. But the next moment the plane was diving to the attack again – nothing could touch him now – and the stern of the senior officer's boat was sticking right out of the water. The plane passed directly above it and dropped four bombs – four direct hits, four water spouts. As they subsided the seas closed over one more sunken U-boat – and every man of its crew.

We had to face it – it was now or never. Our alarm bell rang and we sprang down the hatchway. The Commander gave one last look. "Liberator preparing to attack!" In a twinkling we were back on deck. 'the gun crews rushed to their stations. "Open fire at 3,000 metres!" The enemy once more turned away. To score a hit we would normally have to close the range to 2,000 metres, but we could not wait until then. For, once within range, the plane could only do two things, press home his attack and shoot up our gun-crews or else break off the engagement in order to drop his bombs without interference. When a plane turns away under fire it is almost as good as being shot down. For such action deprives it of its power to use its guns and also exposes the entire length of its fuselage. On the other hand, if we managed to shoot it down before it dropped its bombs, there was always the danger that it might crash aboard, blowing us all to smithereens, and so score a victory at the moment of its own destruction. That risk we had to take, for the tactics we had so far followed only wasted time. It was impossible to dive in the short interval that elapsed between the time the plane turned away and the moment of its next attack.

Then a sudden thought occurred to our Commander. The crews on the conning-tower vanished below, only one staying on deck, and he hid behind the shield of the quadruple AA-gun. The Commander watched from the hatchway, having now changed his white cap for a steel helmet. Everything worked out according to plan – the pilot saw us rush below and dived to attack. Our best shot was waiting for him: when the plane was 2,000 metres away he fired. Hit in the wing, the enemy turned away. Now he would have to circle round before attacking again and that would take time. We seized our chance and dived.

In this terribly tense moment I was on the hatchway ladder. How slowly the time went by, even the depth indicator seemed to have stuck!... 15 fathoms... 20. Then a sharp explosion; it felt as if someone had slashed my hand with a whip. All compartments reported all correct. Heaven be praised! But we thought of the third U-boat that was still surfaced and were sure that it would be sunk.

When we returned to harbour we found that the third boat was in fact overdue. Later, in a prisoner-of-war camp, I met the Commander and heard the rest of the story. Twenty minutes after we dived sixteen planes were on the scene. Three destroyers came in sight and opened up with their guns, while the planes attacked in four groups, in threes and from every quarter simultaneously. The fight was soon over. The gun crews and everyone else on deck were wiped out, and when the U-boat went down only five men were saved. So it had met its fate the fate of so many other U-boats – as we had foreseen.

The flaw in the idea of sending U-boats out in company lay in the assumption that hostile planes over the Bay of Biscay were bound to attack, whereas, on the contrary, they had no need to do so. All they had to do was to prevent the U-boats from diving till more planes or warships that were standing by all over England for emergency calls to the Bay could be called up. At a later stage we realised the need for heavier AA-guns with a range of up to 3 miles to be fitted in U-boats, and in that way we were able to ward off the planes before reinforcements arrived and so gain the essential time to dive.

The British BBC, which had once before announced the destruction of our boat, now broadcast again that we were sunk. We only hoped that our families would not pick it up, although the enemy propaganda transmitter "Calais", which broadcast at regular intervals in German and French, was something they would be likely to tune in to in spite of it being forbidden. Nevertheless in a few days, sometimes dived and sometimes surfaced, we were out of the danger zone.

CHAPTER TEN

NEPTUNE COMES ABOARD

I WAS going to the South Atlantic for the first time, a much more pleasant prospect than the North Atlantic. The climate was far more agreeable and the enemy's defences were weaker. The steamers to be met sailing alone there were easier to attack as it was seldom crossed in convoy. Although most boats cross the equator on the surface we intended to do so dived, and as we were now approaching the line we were working up to a full-scale celebration with daily rehearsals, into which the whole ship's company threw themselves heart and soul. Every evening there was a radio transmission from Neptune's Castle over our "radio network", in other words the submarine's warning telephone installation, and we were entertained by the compositions of improvised "choirs".

The kernel of the entertainment, however, lay in the three degrees of ordeal which have to be undergone when you cross the line. In preparation for these the uninitiated were divided into three sections, and everybody tried to pin something onto someone else to bring him into the lowest category, which naturally added to the general suspense. We had read all about the traditional customs and it was certainly going to be grim if we kept them up. There was keel-hauling, for instance, namely lowering men over one side and dragging them right under the ship to be hauled up on the other. As a boat's keel is not exactly smooth but coated with barnacles, and so on, we could easily imagine what might happen. We had even heard that there had been cases of drowning from clinging to the keel. However, we consoled ourselves by reflecting that we were not living in the barbarous past but in the highly civilised and humane twentieth century.

A day or two before we reached the line a radio report came through announcing that Neptune, his daughter Thetis, with the Chief of Police, Physician-in-ordinary and others of his Court were assembled in the Castle. The Chief of Police's report went something like this:

"I have just sighted a ship approaching our sacred line, apparently without giving due notice of its arrival. I tried to take its name, but in vain. The people on board make a very bad impression, they're all bearded like robber barons."

Neptune: "Unheard-of insolence, they must be severely punished."

Thetis: "It's really too terrible. How can I go riding on my seahorse tomorrow?"

After preliminary instructions for a general ducking, special cases were worked up as follows:

Chief of Police: "Your Majesty will be horrified, but I've just seen a horrible creature in this wretched ship with an odd instrument called a sextant taking the stars out of the sky. He is called the chief quartermaster. I think he should be given a ducking of the third degree."

We all listened anxiously, everybody accepting it meekly enough and no one knowing when his own turn was coming as nothing escaped Neptune.

Chief of Police. "There's one particularly objectionable fellow aboard. He's got a red beard. Had I been afflicted with a red beard I would have implored Your Majesty to give me another head. But this beard is certainly the fruit of his wicked doings – there's no doubt it's bloodstained."

Neptune, "Surely not?"

Chief of Police: "I'm afraid there's no question of it, Your Majesty."

Neptune: "Describe him."

Chief of Police: "It seems even his own shipmates are afraid of him. I've seen them report every day, quite pale and ill-looking. He makes them open their mouths, peers down their gullets, probes them with fearsome instruments and actually makes them swallow pills."

Neptune: "Ordeal number three!"

When the great day came Neptune arrived with all his company, the Chief of Police carrying an enormous sword, and a rating, shaved and painted up with a flaxen tow wig as Thetis in the bloom of youth. The Physician-in-ordinary, in enormous spectacles, picked out the victims according to their category, making them take the ordained number of frightful-tasting pills which they could only just swallow, and spraying a fluid made of vinegar, oil and pepper down their throats. That got quick results, and before long Neptune received an offering rich indeed. Then the uninitiated were examined by the Chief of Police who meted out the appropriate ducking. Next the barber did his job, smearing soap all over our noses, mouths and ears and going over our hair and beards with a pair of wooden shears. After that everybody had to go backwards down the hatchway into a tank filled with water and compressed air and pass through the bilges under the engine-room to come out looking like natives. We jolted into innumerable screws and sharp edges on the way because everything had to be done at high speed so that the ceremony should not last longer than the time allowed – if it did you had to start all over again. Finally we went head first into a herring barrel. Four strong arms packed us all in on top of each other and only let us out when we were nearly suffocated. But this was the signal to end the ordeal. A quick shower, a glass of brandy in celebration, and – we had crossed the line.

A few days later our ship's doctor, the unfortunate victim of ordeal number three, fell ill, complaining of stomachache.

"I knew I should never come back, and now I'm dying," he told us. In sixteen hours his fears were realised.

The sun rose red as blood. The guns were loaded and the Commander made a short speech. A triple salute was fired and in a hammock covered with the German flag we lowered the doctor over the side. Poor man, he really did have a presentiment of death and we did him bitter wrong to make fun of it. One should never meddle with superstitions or the supernatural. In the mood we were in crossing the line we had handled him severely. And the following midnight on the bridge we had heard the cry of a bird, in old sailing ships a foreboding of death on board. After that we never laughed at such things.

Our original plan was to operate off Freetown with eight boats. But two had gone down when we first sailed in company; three more were missing, probably sunk; the sixth had to return to base heavily damaged by bombs and the seventh through lack of fuel. So of all the eight boats assigned to the task only we were fit for action. We did make some tentative attacks, but they were futile, for we were dealing with ships too fast for us to catch. They picked us up with their instruments, showed us their stern and vanished, and soon afterwards the planes came out to hunt us. We were no longer the cat, we were the mouse. Subsequently the shipping route was changed and we had to leave the area. Even if we had been fulfiling the purpose of the High Command by pinning down somebody somewhere we were dissatisfied at our total lack of success. This wasn't war but a sheer struggle for existence.

On our return voyage we surfaced only at night and hugged the coast of Spain just beyond the three-mile limit in waters where there were many fishing-boats from which the enemy radar couldn't distinguish us. Our nerves were on edge, and the slightest sound upset us. We often mistook seagulls – which loom large through binoculars – for oncoming planes. Once we saw a bright light to starboard. In a twinkling a petty officer who was a fine shot had trained his gun on it. The Commander pulled him away.

"Are you mad? It's a lighthouse!"

Luckily it was a long way off and our shells fell short, otherwise the enemy propaganda would have had material enough for a long time to come. "German atrocity. Neutrals bombarded."

This time we had no air escort as we entered St Nazaire, since the Luftwaffe was being used on other fronts, and only two light escort ships put out to meet us. An air-raid was in progress on the base, swarms of four-engined American bombers passing overhead at midday at a height of about 20,000 feet, and the town burning. We saw German fighter-planes pass over – there were flashes, parachutes opened. Here a glove floated in the water, there a boot, Planes were overturning and falling in flames, some exploding in mid-air. "It's all like a film!" exclaimed the junior officer of the watch. "This is the way I like to see war. I always did want to see a real air battle!" Someone, one of our fighter pilots, was swimming in the water and couldn't disentangle himself from his parachute. It was his twenty-fourth birthday and he had just shot down his twenty-fourth plane. He had been awarded the Knight's Cross *(Ritterkreuz)*, had been shot down himself four times and was just going on leave. That was something to celebrate, and we did celebrate it that night. Two days later I went to Paris with him. He had to pick up an old plane and fly it to Berlin for training purposes, so he took me along, and it was certainly a great experience. Though it only took two hours I had to crouch like a rabbit behind the pilot's seat in miserable discomfort.

When we got to Berlin we found that despite all the bomb damage morale was still not at all bad, most of the population being convinced of final victory. The papers were all writing about secret weapons, and every conversation one had came back to that same hopeful subject.

CHAPTER ELEVEN

Awaiting New Weapons

WHEN I rejoined the flotilla everyone started to congratulate me, I couldn't think why.

"You're going to get a Commanding Officer's course," they explained.

My own Commander and chief engineer also left the boat to go on special courses in Germany. Then the inevitable occurred – my boat went to sea and did not return. It was my third escape.

The Flotilla Commander gave a farewell party before we left. We had been longer at St Nazaire than any other submarine. But how many gaps there were in our ranks. The walls of our wardroom were covered with photographs of men who had lost their lives at sea. We made no secret of it; we were proud of them.

The U-boat Commanding Officer's course was held at Neustadt in Holstein. We used a model conning-tower in which all gear was exactly reproduced. Then we went to Danzig for practical instruction and for our skill to be put to the test; we had day and night exercises with dummy torpedoes and got very little sleep. When we passed out they gave us three choices – we could either relieve a Commander on active service, take command of a training boat, or take over a new submarine. Active service was sheer suicide in those days, but ashore we could contact old friends and wait till new types of U-boat came into production. Admiral Dönitz spoke about the position at some length, giving us to understand very clearly that experienced officers were being withdrawn from the Atlantic to take over the new types. I wanted to be appointed to a new boat from the Blohm and Voss yard in Hamburg, but it did not work out as I anticipated, for the High Command had other plans and I went to No. 21 flotilla at Pillau.

There were thirty-six U-boats there used exclusively for training new entries. My boat was U-148, Type IID, which with its 300 tons displacement was the latest model of this class, whose limited range and slow speed made them unsuitable for active service. Fundamentally they were constructed along the same lines as the larger boats but there was less room on board, the whole ship's company, including the Commander, taking their meals in the fo'c's'le, it was much harder work because there were fewer men with just as much to do. Everybody kept a six-hour watch and had six hours off duty, if you can call it that. There was no privacy for the Commander. Everybody could see exactly what I was doing and notice all my idiosyncrasies, such as exactly how long I slept and whether I snored and how many times a day I washed and when I put a clean shirt on. As Commander, I was responsible for everything that went on aboard, having to administer punishment and make all decisions – I realised now that I was no longer young, although in 1943 I was only twenty-three. But there were only two alternatives: either I was fit to take over one of the many U-boats we were promised or else I was going to be turned out.

I found it particularly trying to give a lecture twice a week as the High Command laid down. An hour's talk involves a lot of reading, and I had to work it up at night as I really hadn't the time otherwise. When I had to touch on the military situation I found it quite impossible to disguise its gravity by twisting things or churning out propaganda. Yet I could not leave the men dispirited. I was in no position to judge whether we had lost the war or not, or whether a workable political solution existed for Germany. Whatever enemy propaganda may say, a serviceman cannot turn traitor to his country – his one golden rule is to stand fast and obey orders. It was no business of ours to dabble in politics. As long as we were at war we had to go on fighting, obey our superiors, maintain discipline and suppress mutiny with all the means in our power – the Allies had to do the same. After all, I had to train my men for U-boat service and what use would they be if their morale was low? A tiny cog like the ordinary individual cannot possibly grasp the import of the immense events taking place around him, and has not history always honoured the fighting-man, from the Spartans to Napoleon's armies, even when he did fight for a lost cause or one that many have thought wrong?

We were still turning out U-boat crews in large numbers, and there was another flotilla like our own at Gotenhafen. The plans for expanding our service were excellent, the course being divided into two parts, practical and theoretical. The theoretical side we taught in lecture-rooms ashore, where seamen, petty officers, chief petty officers and officers were all lectured on U-boat warfare together. The permanent complements in the training-boats were kept as low as possible, the new entries taking up their practical duties on board in rotation, as you can't understand a complicated affair like a U-boat till you have handled its mechanism yourself and learnt the correct words of command on the spot. During their six months' exercises in the Baltic they studied how to apply their knowledge, but it usually took them several operations to master it, provided of course they were still alive! Naturally it wasn't much fun for the instructors to go to sea with new entries on board. Our responsibilities were heavy. During the year that I spent on exercises in the Baltic we lost four submarines, though we were never allowed to dive for more than two hours in prescribed areas where every conceivable precaution was taken.

I shall always be proud of my own ship's company – we beat all safety records, and, moreover, there was a genuine bond between us. I knew everybody's Christian name and background. Our mutual trust was such that, accepting an idea from my petty officer, I allowed Schnapps on board. They, like the rest of us, would have preferred to get a little more to drink than regulations prescribed, since in winter the temperature in the Baltic is usually about 20 degrees below zero and the steel bridge is permanently covered with ice. There we would stand without any protection for four hours on end, frozen to the marrow. After that there's nothing like a good glass of hot grog. I gave permission, knowing very well that if I were denounced in the right quarter the consequences would be highly unpleasant.

The team spirit in the Navy was unique, especially among our year. We had our own code and anyone who offended against it was boycotted. We even decided whom to recommend for promotion to officers, for here we had the right of veto. We had our own magazine which reported everything that went on, in particular the award of special mentions and decorations. In 1944 it proposed a reunion in East Prussia, and hard as it was at that time we somehow did arrange it and everybody who could possibly come did so. It wasn't easy to secure hotel rooms, but we did that too – everything was laid on on a lavish scale. We even had feminine company, a varied selection of ballet dancers, actresses, schoolgirls and family friends – you can't make a party go without them! There were more than two hundred of us and we ended up with a visit to the Opera and a tour round Königsberg. There were fellows from the Fleet Air Arm, from patrol boats, minesweepers, torpedo-boats, destroyers, capital ships and submarines stationed in nearly every country in Europe. How everyone had changed! A few years ago we had been boys; now we were men with great responsibilities.

My Flotilla Commander was a Captain who had won the Knight's Cross at the beginning of the war for sinking an aircraft carrier. We all had confidence in his straightforward manner and in his abhorrence of speech-making and morale-boosting. He was quite frank with all Commanders about Germany's critical situation, and told us that nothing save the production of new and decisive weapons would save us from defeat. Everybody was talking about these new secret weapons, and it was thought to be quite certain that work on new kinds of construction was going on all over the country. But we should have done all this at the beginning of the war and acted with greater foresight then instead of being so over-optimistic as we were after the campaign in the West. To think that after the fall of France part of our industrial plant was actually switched to peacetime production! Now that the war had reached a critical phase our problem was to turn out new and decisive weapons for the fighting services in sufficient quantities before it was too late, in a neck-and-neck race against time. Our industry, as we could see, was suffering from the effect of unremitting Allied air-raids, and continually there were disastrous delays and a general falling-off in production. Yet, certain as they were that a turn for the better must come, both the civil population and the services were quite surprisingly confident. Primarily this was due to the soldierly German temperament, but it was bolstered up by the way our propaganda service handled the idea of new secret weapons. Pamphlets and newsletters accessible only to a limited circle dealt with such problems as "How can we win?" and "What are the means?" in a really masterly fashion. There were excellent articles about the general principles governing the new technical weapons and photostats of foreign papers and technical journals which led us to conclude that many highly effective devices had already been tried out – high-speed guided missiles which had actually been seen in flight, and a new type of aircraft completely different from anything we were accustomed to. By publishing the enemy's warnings to his own people to be on guard against surprises from the German side they enhanced the general effect. As all these publications were on the secret list we were naturally very keen to read them. It's a fundamental trait of human nature to derive pleasure and a sense of importance from feeling you belong to a privileged caste which is really in the know and in a position to drop hints to the less well-informed. By this means, therefore, rumours of decisive weapons filtered through to the mass of the people, so that if a conversation turned on our bleak prospects someone was sure to burst in and say that people who talked like that obviously didn't know what they were blathering about, hadn't they heard that... the wish is often father to the thought.

Anyway, many doubters plucked up courage again – we were simply going to win the war with some sort of new secret weapon and anybody who didn't realise that was obviously ignorant of the enormous strides we had made in technical warfare. So that was that.

Regularly every three months Admiral Dönitz came round to encourage us in our work. He used to make rousing speeches, and it was a pretty safe bet that he would wind up with the words "We shall pursue this war till final victory is achieved". After parade he often stayed another day with our flotilla and spent the evening with the Commanders of the training-boats. I often sat next to him and he always left me with the same impression of a reliable and energetic man perfectly confident that final victory *would* be achieved. He met all criticisms by short, clipped references to ultramodern U-boats that could do quite fabulous things – ever since April 1944 two of these U-boats had been launched every day, which meant sixty every month and seven hundred and twenty a year. He argued that if he couldn't judge the situation, then nobody could. He was continually seeing Hitler, and the feeling at headquarters was one of complete confidence, and rightly so. The Luftwaffe were trying out new prototypes, and very soon we should see a complete turn of the tide in our favour, but we must just hold on for the moment. He also promised training-boat Commanders the command of the first new U-boats; we had acquired so much experience in our daily training manoeuvres, apart from being the few surviving officers who had been on active service since 1941, that he had deliberately relieved us of our jobs in operational U-boats to entrust us with these new submarines. Naturally we were pleased. Whenever he visited us he left us feeling better, and despite the gloomy present we looked forward hopefully to the future. He was our Commanding Officer, he had directed submarine warfare successfully till the end of 1942, and, unlike certain other public figures, he had not put his sons into safe jobs.

In order to describe these so-called revolutionary developments I must explain that a U-boat generally has four sets of propulsive machinery: two Diesel engines and two electric motors, of which it uses the first when surfaced and the second when dived. That is obviously far from being a perfect arrangement since the ship can only use half its available power at a time, while the rest is sheer ballast. If somebody could only discover a type of engine equally suitable for surface and underwater work, an engine that worked without batteries, then our potentialities would increase enormously, enabling us, for one thing, to achieve higher speeds underwater. Dived, we could only reach a maximum of about nine knots, less rather than more, at which speed our current ran out in two hours (normally we would cruise at three knots to spare the batteries), but surfaced we could keep up 18 knots indefinitely on our Diesels.

A mechanical engineer called Walther had discovered the ideal solution when he invented a turbine that ran on special fuel. The essential thing about the Walther engine was that it did not rely on atmospheric air but obtained its essential oxygen from tanks of hydrogen peroxide. This was a U-boat Commander's dream. It is sad for a German to look back now and reflect on how it might have affected the fortunes of war had we not discovered it too late.

All our submarine experts met at a resort in the Harz mountains to devise a U-boat best fitted for Walther engines. The answer was a boat about twice the size of our ordinary 600-ton operational type, built to dive to 150 fathoms, whereas our ordinary models were designed for 50 fathoms only. (At the end of the war we were doing 140 fathoms, and one ship actually achieved 180.) It was established, however, that the existing Walther prototype engine was only suitable for a small boat, and the production of larger units was beset with difficulties. An intermediate solution was found, by which, although the installation of Walther units had to be dropped, the new construction hulls could be used with electric motors of considerably greater efficiency.

At this time new submarines were first fitted with a Snorchel or "Snort" (frequently misspelt Schnorkel or Schnörkel) a north-German dialect term for nose. The Dutch had fitted their submarines with an air intake back in 1940, but they had only used it to ventilate their ships, while the German Snort, raised and lowered by hydraulic pressure, enabled us to use our internal combustion engines under water and so solved our most serious problem. A U-boat could now cruise dived for the whole period until its fuel gave out, and was thus equipped with the answer to Radar.

The new intermediate type fitted with Snorchel was known as Type XXI. It was of streamlined hull-form and designed as a true submarine, not just a "submersible" like the older types. Its underwater speed was in consequence 16 knots, which could be kept up for long periods, and it was fitted with six bow-tubes, with twelve spare torpedoes stowed abaft them. This arrangement enabled it to fire a salvo of six torpedoes, reload, fire, reload and fire again, discharging its full outfit of 18 fish inside 15 minutes. A new type rangefinder, furthermore, enabled the Type XXI boats to fire torpedoes at a depth of 50 metres, without using the periscope at all.

But for the enemy the worst threat came from our new acoustic torpedoes. These differ from the normal electric torpedoes by having a very complicated listening-device coupled to the rudder-mechanism. We could fire this type of tinfish without even seeing our objectives or estimating their range, since as soon as it was fired from the tube it circled around while the U-boat dived to greater depths to get out of its way. It then made straight off in the direction from which the sounds of ships screws emanated, and struck aft where the engines and steering apparatus were located.

The listening-device was so sensitive that it could pick up a ship lying stopped, by the noise of its auxiliary machinery. In one month during 1944 eighty enemy destroyers and corvettes were sunk by these fantastic torpedoes. It came to the point when, just after we had started using them, the enemy U-boat chasers had literally to break off attacking our submarines, as it had become nothing less than suicidal for them. Later on the Allies devised various counter-devices, but they were not completely effective.

CHAPTER TWELVE

My Last Command

AT CHRISTMAS 1944 I took command of a new submarine, U-977. It was the normal class but fitted with a Snort. The new heavy submarines by which we had set such store were still not available, the strain on German industry being so great that their construction had to be postponed. The land attack from West and East simultaneously had been proving too much for the German Army even before the great disaster on the Eastern front came in January 1945. When it did come we had to evacuate the base at Pillau and transfer it to Wesermünde, taking our base-ship with us in our retreat. Bitter as it was to have to say goodbye to East Prussia, which we had come to love, it was clear that we were defeated, and that our only hope now lay in a line-up with the West against Communism. Our leaders clung to that hope as a drowning man clutches at a straw, but there was not the slightest sign that the Anglo-Americans were prepared to entertain the idea.

At heart I revolted against the useless prolonging of the war, and I was infuriated at the thought of incompetent, cowardly civilians sending boys and old men into action while they themselves broke every promise they had ever made. But I was a serving officer and I had no intention of breaking faith. I took it for granted that I must not leave my fellow countrymen in the lurch but stand by them to the very end. My Flotilla Commander had put me in charge of a convoy escort consisting of four U-boats, which we safely reassembled at Wesermünde. We were still training men for the service, which struck me as sheer lunacy when so many trained U-boat men whose boats had been sunk by bombs in harbour were fighting on land.

In April 1946 U-977 was pronounced seaworthy, at any rate in the eyes of people who didn't have to go to sea in her, although in my view she was not fit for active service in any respect whatever. I had proposed a change of batteries as the existing ones were only running at 70 per cent efficiency and the renewal of certain parts, armour-plating for the conning-tower, fresh radio equipment and a minimum period for training the crew, since some of the ratings were quite without experience. However, I was told that my request for improvements had been rejected for want of material, and ordered to proceed to Kiel to embark stores. I had no choice. But I owed it to my men to drive home any arguments while I could, and I only hoped the Admiral would understand our position.

A few hours after our arrival at Kiel I went aboard the depot-ship and happened to arrive while a political pep-talk was going on. The speaker concluded, without any logical argument, that final victory was assured. He seemed to impress the Admiral. When the talk was over, I requested an interview with Dönitz, and being invited into his cabin, I spoke my mind.

"My dear Schaeffer," he replied' "you know very well we shall fight on till victory. We shall win whatever the cost. I see from your decorations that you are a veteran, and if you can't go to sea, who can?"

The conclusion was that whether my boat was seaworthy or not I must take her to sea. I made no comment.

Shortly afterwards I went to Berlin for a few days to say goodbye to my mother. The war was rapidly nearing its end and plans were being made to defend Hamburg, but no one among the planners seemed to care what was going to happen to the German people. This was what the mad demand for unconditional surrender was leading to...

It took twenty-four hours to reach Berlin – we had air-raid warnings at regular intervals and took cover underneath the train till it could go on again. Next to me sat an SS officer who, in spite of my flatly contradicting him, simply would not stop talking about decisive new secret weapons. I was fed up with secret weapons by now for I knew perfectly well from my own experience that if all the blueprints were there so were the air-raids on our factories. "Well, of course, you aren't really in a position to judge," he said, but he was, naturally, because he *was* working at some SS HQ or other and was out watching the tests every day. If I would only come and look him up I would see something that would make me sit up.

When I got to Berlin I really did look him up, and after I had waited at the HQ entrance for some time my new acquaintance appeared and started showing me round. Everybody there was certain we were going to win, with a conviction I'd never seen the like of even after the fall of France. Among the fantastic contrivances of which I was shown photographs was one called a death ray which my friend wanted me to come back and see in action next day.

But I wasn't wasting any more time. I wanted to see my mother, for it was obvious the Russians were advancing on Berlin and that the last battle was going to be fought there. The city was being transformed into a fortress, with tramcars overturned and barricades going up everywhere. I wanted to get my mother away, but she said she meant to stay in Berlin at all costs; she would manage the Russians all right, she said. And so she did.

I returned to Kiel. Every day a hail of bombs poured down onto the town, and several times a day I had to take my boat out to some sheltered inlet on the coast. The drone of aircraft never stopped, but we never saw a German fighter in the sky.

Two days before we were due to go to sea with our boat "ready for service" there came at midday the screech of sirens warning of another raid, and we cast off as usual. In my wake I had a U-boat commanded by a man of my own year. Proceeding in close formation, as we were practically in Kiel harbour, we were right in among the bombs, American planes whirring overhead one after the other. They knew that we had no AA defences any longer and so they took no heed of risks. About a hundred yards away two bombs landed on the passenger ship *New York* in which I had travelled to America not so long ago, and she flared up like a torch. Ammunition was blowing up all round us – it was altogether a fiendish display of fireworks. The next moment there was an explosion just astern of us and I gave the order full speed ahead, though it really couldn't make the slightest difference at what speed we travelled, but it calms a man's nerves to give an order of some kind. My contemporary's boat astern of us received a direct hit and went down in a few seconds. There weren't many survivors.

At last, several days later, we were able to start for Norway, where our instructions were to refuel, try out our Snort for a couple of days, and then proceed on active operations. Three U-boats in all were detailed for the task and one of them was of the new XXI class, the first to be detailed for action. I put into a Danish port on the way, which wasn't exactly part of the programme but there was no need to be over-particular. In Denmark there was still plenty to eat and we could apply to the German naval stores there. The more food we took aboard the better.

The inspector was a kind-hearted old soul and certainly not mean, a very different type from the hidebound chief victualling officer at Pillau who carried out his instructions to the letter instead of using his common sense, with the result that an enormous quantity of stores fell into enemy hands. Practically all we had to do was point to the things we wanted to get them. My men brought kegs of butter and hams and eggs and pretty well every imaginable eatable on board. The engineer was already getting worried about overloading, which would make it harder to surface, but we reckoned there was still a pretty good margin and sent one more lorry round to the stores. It was always a comfort to be sure we wouldn't run out in any foreseeable time,

The Commander of the Type XXI job kept prattling about the wonders of his new boat, and even if he hadn't done so I would have been naturally envious as it was a really wonderful piece of workmanship. Out of sheer irritation I bet him a cask of champagne I'd reach the coast of Norway before he did. It was the last bet I made in the Navy. Our orders were to proceed from Denmark to Norway submerged and a Type XXI U-boat dived had a cruising speed of around eight knots whereas ours could only do three knots. At the most he could work up to 18 knots while we could only manage something between eight and nine knots for one hour, or two at most.

The Norwegian passage was considered extremely dangerous as the British kept a close lookout in those waters. They knew quite well that every warship leaving Germany would have to pass that way, since we had virtually lost all our bases in France. Over half our boats were lost on that run, largely because it was impossible to dive under air attack owing to the whole area being sown with minefields.

Almost immediately after we had parted company our Radar located enemy aircraft, twelve of them, or so we estimated, bearing down on us at a hair-raising speed. Just then we were in shallow mine-sown waters, and from the sound they were all around us, either about to attack at once or else gathering preparatory to swooping. At this date the enemy was using new rockets, whose full blast we would no doubt get since they didn't explode at water level but only at a certain depth and so could be used effectively against a submarine in the act of diving These rockets blew a hole three inches across and no submarine could stand up to that. They were also much more accurate than an ordinary bomb.

I had had my fill of air-attacks at night, with the gun-crews dazzled by parachute flares, and unable to make out the attacking planes, which always kept well above the flares. We would only hear the familiar disquieting hum of the engines, and having tracer bullets flying all round you and bombs exploding in the dark is not a pleasant sensation – there's no way to hit back. I knew that if we were still surfaced when they attacked, our number would be up, so I had to take a chance and dive. Luckily we didn't hit any mines.

Every time we raised our search receiver above the surface it indicated aircraft Radar very close, so it seemed that they had picked up our course and were in hot pursuit. We had to wait till daybreak before we could try out our Snort, which was quite unfamiliar to the engineer and to many of the crew – this was the reason why I had gone on my short course in the Baltic under one of my superior officers.

Morale on board was not too bad. We had escaped the general chaos by being at sea, for had our boat happened to have been sunk we should all have been posted to the Army, which was the last thing any of us wanted. As for me, well, I was my own master, and in my own boat, and all the crew stood by me.

After we had got through the worst minefield we were able to proceed without worrying at 25 fathoms. Eventually the time came to recharge our batteries, which was our chance to try out our Snort. There was no need to surface, for thanks to the Snort we could now use our Diesels under water, and it is very hard to pick up the top of a Snort by Radar. We were cruising at ten fathoms now and I wanted to make sure there were no ships or planes about. Sometimes they would keep a look-out for U-boats without using Radar, so I gave orders to go up to seven fathoms, namely Snort depth. There was nothing in sight so we started up the engines, one to charge the batteries and the other to drive the boat.

We were now making a good seven knots. A stream of air was coming in through the Snort but the pressure inside the boat dropped considerably. The suction of the engines was too great, and the engineer wasn't doing his job. At one moment the Snort was up too high and at the next it had dipped below the surface. It was no good going on that way, for when the Snort dips, the air intake shuts automatically and the essential air for the Diesels is sucked out of the engine-room. Finally we got the Snort working better, but our internal pressure kept changing as the Snort valve snapped down and flew open at short intervals. Our ears were aching, this Snort business was uncanny. I lost my temper and began to swear, though it was unfair to blame the engineer, who was making his first passage with the thing. But that didn't help much because if by any chance there happened to be a plane overhead the airmen weren't going to stop bombing us just to give us a chance to get more practice with our Snort.

So we went along like a great sea-serpent, surfacing diving, surfacing and diving once again. We were now down to 15 fathoms, and by the time the Diesels had been sucking in air from the engine room for hard on a minute, our eyes were popping out and our eardrums nearly bursting. The whole thing was simply unbearable. At this depth the exhaust gases couldn't escape because the water pressure had risen too high, so the gases were forced back into the engine-room, all black and suffocating and smothering the place with smoke. Everybody rushed out of the engine-room blinded and with tears streaming from their eyes. Some chaps put on their escape apparatus, then stripped it all off again and gave it up. The whole boat was black with smoke and it was quite impossible to distinguish any object on board. Everyone was groping vaguely about in the fog.

"Surface!" Having given the order, I climbed up the ladder to the conning-tower hatch, feeling seriously worried as I staggered up in case any of the crew should become unconscious before we could open the blowing valves. But at last the compressed air came hissing into our tanks and the boat rose quickly to the surface. According to all the textbooks the air pressure should be regulated very slowly, but the men not unnaturally had only one thought in their minds, which was to get up into the fresh air – just the way I felt myself in fact. In a moment we were through the hatch and up on deck. Everybody was gasping and many were holding their hands to their ears, which were aching terribly because we had risen too quickly.

Meanwhile the officer of the watch and I scanned the horizon. There was nothing in sight and we could breathe freely again – it was the first time I had ever surfaced without smoking a cigarette, and that speaks volumes. Our orders ran: "Proceed to Norway submerged, and use the Snort. These are particularly dangerous waters", but it wasn't so easy to carry out such orders with people who had never had any experience with the Snort. Actually there had been nowhere to train them, as the Baltic was no longer considered safe for naval exercises, but we were to be allowed two days' training when we arrived in Norway.

Accordingly after we had ventilated the boat I made up my mind not to dive again, at any rate with the Snort, as I had no inclination to be gassed like a rat in a trap, but to make another effort with the thing when we got to Norway.

The view from the bridge was magnificent, brilliant sunshine without a cloud in the sky. We were not likely to be taken unawares in that sort of weather, so whatever the orders were I thought that the best and quickest way was to carry on to Norway surfaced. Incidentally, it was also the surest way to win my bet and the cask of champagne, because I was now making 18 knots on the surface and the Type XXI submarine was only doing nine knots submerged. Nothing went wrong this time. Two planes were reported but they were a long way off and couldn't see us. We knew they were not using Radar from our listening device. I saw no reason why they should, as I felt quite sure that they were carrying out their routine patrol duties without keeping any special look-out for U-boats, because no U-boats had been cruising surfaced in the area for some time and we usually only used the Snort at night. The air-crews would certainly know that, so why should they strain themselves for nothing? If we saw them approaching any nearer we would have time to dive before they could attack with any chance of success. In fact they passed us about 6,000 metres away.

On 26th April 1945 we put into the base at Christiansund South. I won my champagne because neither of the other U-boats arrived till the 27th.

We were now ready for operations. One mild night of that northern spring I bivouacked with all the crew on a mountain slope. We had lit a log fire and the flames blazed scarlet against the sky, the sparkling stars and shimmering sea. The massive rocks of the cyclopean scene have made that place for ever vivid in my memory. We lay in a circle round the fire, forty-eight of us in all, talking of the troubled days in our own country and the fate of our families and friends. The cup passed round all right, for we weren't short of drink, but there was no laughing or singing to break the silence of the northern night. Our thoughts were too heavy for that. A few days ago my engineer had learnt of his father's death. He had lost an arm in the First World War only to be killed serving with the Volksturm in the Second. Germany, the mighty nation of only three years ago, was now defeated and broken, with foreign troops pouring over her countryside.

Finally the fire died down. Our last party ashore was over. The next day we should be going to sea.

While we were at Christiansund Admiral Dönitz broadcast a proclamation that there was no question of surrender, but, all the same, the fatal collapse did follow immediately afterwards. Hitler had been killed in the battle of Berlin and as Dönitz was C-in-C of all armed forces as well as now head of the state, everyone said he would carry on the war from Norway. Meanwhile the 2nd of May had come, and as we were due to sail with our usual complement, the Flotilla Commander made one last effort to rouse us in a farewell speech which ended with the words "Fight on to the very end – Germany will never, never surrender."

So, using our Snort at night, we left the coast of Norway behind us, with orders to lie off Southampton Water and if possible go into the harbour and do what damage we could.

A few days after we had sailed our main periscope collapsed. This was serious, as we now had no choice but to use the Snort, and with the Snort we had to travel blind. Planes might pounce on us, U-boat chasers hound us down, but we could see nothing of what was happening on the surface. True, we carried a reserve periscope, but that didn't help us out as it was a short type, designed only for use when we attacked at night or in the twilight. The glass was a special one and through it we could only see what lay directly on top of us. Come what might, however, I was not putting back into harbour, and so we inflexibly pursued our southward course dived.

Our nerves were strained to breaking point when we cruised in this way by Snort. I know of nothing worse than travelling blind, in virtually total ignorance of what is going on on the surface. Worse still, this was the season when the days in northern Europe begin to draw out and the nights grow lighter. We of course used the darkest hours to surface and charge our batteries, but all night long the Snort trailed its plume of white steam, and when, as sometimes happened, it exhaled a column of black smoke as well we were a still more obvious mark for enemy attack.

Of course we had our Radar search aerial on our Snort, but for all we knew it might be obsolete and might not be picking up all wavelengths. For a long time during the last months of the war continuous air attack had held up our production and it was quite on the cards that the Allies might be using new gear now. Even with a Snort a periscope is really indispensable as in the last resort there is no technical device that can replace the human eye.

It was unfortunate for us that it is never really dark in these northern waters. We might be spotted by the smoke trail of the Snort, and we never knew how much that smoke needed controlling as we had no periscope to see it with. If it had been dark it wouldn't have mattered, for then you can't make out smoke easily, but when it is light it betrays you miles away. It had betrayed many ships to us in our time and we had sunk them all. If any ship or plane approached without using Radar that our search receiver could pick up or without using Radar at all we would know nothing. about it. A passing warship could even lasso us by catching our Snort in a strand of wire! We were like a blind man picking his way across a country full of wild beasts with only his sense of bearing to help him, and whose only hope is that the beasts will roar.

On top of it all the noise of our Diesels underwater made it impossible for us to use our hydrophones, and so we lost our last means of knowing whether enemy ships were trying to pick us up with Radar. Practically every ship that used these waters was a warship and we all knew how strictly the enemy kept watch on the approaches through which every U-boat had to pass to get to the Atlantic. Their main chance obviously being to trap us in the narrows before we could get out into the open sea.

We now seemed to be in the middle of the ring of the enemy's blockade. Whenever we could use our search receiver, that is to say whenever "snorting" or surfaced, we caught the typical dull hum of radar transmissions as they first swelled and then died away, our warning light flashing light green, now clear, now faint. When the enemy was trying to pick up German craft he trained his aerial with a steady circular rotation, and when the waves from his Radar transmitter contacted the search-receiver aerial mounted on our Snort we saw the reactions distinctly – an experienced wireless operator can sometimes even tell whether his craft has been picked up or not. The wisest course for us was to dive deep and house our Snort, which at first we always did. But the upshot was that we never had time enough to charge our batteries. Not only that, we were also perpetually using up current by always proceeding deep underwater, which meant subsequently taking six hours to recharge instead of three; and by then it would be daylight. What with this and continually waiting for a bomb to fall we felt as if we were standing on the edge of a volcano. This went on day after day, always in the dark as we had no current to spare for light below, and never had the natural light of the sun since we didn't dare to surface. In our free moments we were always thinking of when we could next attempt to use the Snort, and yet we were always fearful that it mightn't work. We were only too conscious that the old type of U-boat like ours nearly always failed to return, even when it was fitted with a Snort and the periscope was in working order.

This agony of suspense went on for five days. British propaganda had recently estimated a U-boat's life at forty days, and this time it was right and we knew it. Forty days was generous. Well, we had been at sea for eight altogether now so there should be thirty-two to go. Of course, it didn't follow that there would be thirty-two, it might happen tonight, or tomorrow, still, we were hoping for the best. While we were groping through with our Snort my junior watchkeeper brought me a signal from headquarters which ran roughly like this:

To all men of the Submarine Service. For five years you have fought gallantly on all the seven seas. You can look back with pride on what you have achieved. You have done such deeds as were never accomplished before and never will be equalled in the future. You have made history yet in spite of all you have endured the worst still lies ahead. Tomorrow we surrender, and from tomorrow you will take all your orders from the Allied Command.

We didn't pick up the speaker's name because the aerial attached to our Snort broke before we got so far. Who was it who had been speaking? Surely not Dönitz, after all his fine words? No, it was probably an enemy trap they must have decoded our cypher and picked up our wavelength. I discussed its possible meaning with my officers. It seemed out of the question that Dönitz as head of the state should have ordered unconditional surrender. What was it he had said the last time we saw him? "We shall fight to the very last man. We shall never, never surrender." We thought the Allies might have broken down our final stand by their overwhelming numerical superiority in the last few days, but I couldn't conceive it possible that our own leaders had sunk so far as to send out official orders to surrender. I went back to my cabin to think things over alone – I knew I must make a decision, but my head was in a whirl.

Next day we picked up another signal, which I again felt must come from the enemy since it was quite irreconcilable with the outlook and the temper of our own leaders and completely at variance with our last orders. I decided to ignore it and to act on my own initiative. Finally there came a third signal to all U-boats at sea to surface, put their armament out of action and hoist blue or white flags – from the Allied Disarmament Commission. I could stand it no longer and gave orders to shut off the wireless as it was no longer able to convey the true views of our own leaders but was now merely serving the ends of a ruthless enemy.

At this point I decided to take the crew into my confidence – they had been kept in the dark too long and I now spoke to them openly more or less as follows:

"*Kameraden*. It seems that the darkest hour has struck both for us and for Germany. We have lost the Second World War. We all know what lies before the German people – the enemy propaganda has made no secret of it. I am thinking of the Morgenthau plan to convert all Germany into pastures for goats and to sterilise all German males. The foundations of a policy built on hatred have been laid. German women and German girls lie helplessly exposed to the lust of the armies of occupation while their menfolk are deported. In vain have our leaders, of whom the last was Admiral Dönitz, implored the enemy to spare the German people for the sake of the future of Europe. But their hatred is too bitter, a hatred not of Nazism as they have pretended – for Nazism ended with the death of Hitler – but of the people of Germany themselves.

"We must decide the right course to take. We can either hoist the white flag, or sink our boat, or put into harbour in some country that has behaved honourably all through the war. One of our engineers knows Argentina and has kept in touch with friends there, so he is well informed about this South American republic, and I myself have friends and acquaintances there. It has a great future from all I know I believe it to be the most progressive state in South America, with its vast natural resources and undeveloped areas where the individual has every chance to make a career for himself.

"*Kameraden*, the enemy demands that we surrender, asserting that our leaders have capitulated. In view of everything that has happened I do not think it likely that Admiral Dönitz has ever formally surrendered, It may be that our resistance has been broken by the enemy fighting on German soil, at a hundred-to-one odds, but there can be no question of our accepting orders from him without knowing more of the circumstances. I suggest, therefore, that we continue on our way, but that we do not attack a single ship, for I would not have us revenge ourselves with the blood of innocent men. It is futile to carry on the war alone. As it is, we have all the stores we need for our voyage to Argentina to spare us the bitter bread of captivity."

After I had finished speaking they began hammering it all out and separating into various groups. I did not hurry them. When the vote was taken, thirty out of the forty-eight plumped for South America, two wanted to go to Spain, hoping to make a surer and speedier return from there, and sixteen expressed a wish to return to their families – these last married men, nearly all of them petty officers, the oldest on board. Democracy demands that the will of the majority prevail, but in order to meet the wishes of the married men I proposed to land them in Norway, from which they would perhaps be able to make their way home. We could, of course, have entered some harbour or other where the lights would have helped us, but the idea of being at once made prisoners did not attract us. Accordingly we made for a lonely stretch of mountain coast not far from Bergen, there to put them ashore in rubber dinghies by night.

The night of 10th May was an inky one. We hadn't surfaced for eight days and did not precisely know where we were. Navigation in unknown waters is hard enough at the best of times, but particularly in Norwegian waters with their innumerable offshore rocks. Detailed charts are really indispensable, but as we had none we just had to risk it. The petty officers got ready, packed their essentials in their kitbags and worked out their plans with the aid of some large-scale land maps we had. For these men it would probably be the last time they surfaced in a submarine. We were a few miles from shore and the dark foggy night made it hard for us to find our bearings, but we were able to pump up two collapsible rubber dinghies. Every man carried a one-man dinghy on his back as well, and all the gear lay ready on deck including food to last them a month.

When midnight came dawn was already not far away – it was lucky for us this wasn't midsummer or it would have been light already. Even now we hadn't much time, yet we had to go slowly, for the coast here was particularly treacherous. Still, so far so good. Our gauge indicated a depth of 50 fathoms and we were five miles offshore. We went in further... three miles... two miles. The coast drew nearer and the water grew calmer, but we had to go still further inshore than this – we couldn't disembark our friends so far from the coast, for the wind was against them and they could hardly have covered any distance in their dinghies in choppy waters and against the tide. It was a fair certainty they would have been blown out to sea, and there was no possible salvation for them if that happened, at any rate not in the sense they understood it – that of making their way home safely and undetected.

The waters were getting very shallow... five fathoms...

four fathoms... seven fathoms... The reports kept changing as we felt our way gingerly inshore using our electric motors, one going half-speed ahead, and the other ready to go all out astern. Would we pull it off? In spite of everything we imagined we would, since it struck us as highly unlikely that anyone in these parts would be on the look-out for a German submarine.

The next moment the boat began to keel over ever so slightly, for somewhere we had grazed her keel. But we had to go on. We couldn't dream of disembarking the men here, with still a mile or so to go, perhaps a mile and a quarter. We were by now proceeding at one knot only, the slowest we could do, and that only thanks to our electric motors, for the Diesels couldn't do less than six knots.

And then!

The bows just heaved out of the water without any noise and without any sense of shock, the depth gauge still showing two and a half fathoms under the control-room. "Emergency full speed astern!" – but it was too late for that now. Our boat was up over the waterline as far as the for'ard hydroplanes, at a sharp angle, 30 degrees perhaps.

For five minutes the motors went full speed astern, but the boat just would not budge. Then we went ahead on one and astern on the other, but that didn't work either. Our position seemed hopeless.

I suggested to the sixteen men who were going ashore that they should disembark at once before we were discovered. We were bound to be sighted at first light and then we should have to make up our minds whether to blow up our submarine or hand it over intact to the enemy, though there was still time to think that over, for it wasn't light yet.

So we all shook hands for the last time, and that with deep emotion. Yet, after all, the time had to come for all of us to part, as much for those who stayed aboard as for those who went ashore. Oh yes, the time was bound to come when each and all of us would have to fight to fined a living, and we knew the fight wasn't going to be easy.

And so we launched the rubber dinghies. One of them unfortunately capsized, for we lay at too steep an angle, and two men fell into the sea. They were hauled in again, but there was no time for them to change their clothing, for now we could unmistakably make out the first flicker of the dawn.

The next moment the dinghies were moving away, leaving us looking after them and at each other. Maybe their case was happier than ours, aground out here on a rock. Anyhow, the engineer tried this and that to relieve our predicament. We pumped water out of the levelling tanks, setting our trim first to starboard and then to port, and working our engines full speed till the spray from our propeller splashed right over the stern, but all for nothing, the boat simply would not budge an inch. Every minute brought the danger nearer. There was half an hour till the dawn proper, but then our number would be definitely up – a warship would come up, and we would be marched off to the prisoner-of-war cage that would spell the end of liberty for us.

Nevertheless there was one hope left. Our compressed-air bottles were still full, the pressure gauges showing 205 kilograms. The boat might be raised above the rock if we opened the blowing valves suddenly and let compressed air stream through the diving tanks and underneath the keel. So we opened the valves at the bottom and closed those at the top and fervently hoped to get afloat that way.

Compressed air hissed into all tanks! The engines roared to their shrillest pitch ...emergency full speed astern! No one took any notice of the red danger needles on the dials of our instruments.

To us up on the bridge it was obvious how enormous was the strain. The whole boat was throbbing now, hard astarboard, hard a-port! At last she's budging, beginning to move astern, thank heaven, and the bows coming down!

So we turned on our keel. Our navigator had laid off our course and it lay directly astern of us. First slowly, and then with gradually increasing speed, we moved away – as with every moment the coastline emerged more clearly from the darkness. We could dimly make out our shipmates signalling with lights. They had reached the shore and were flashing out a farewell message *Bon voyage. If they catch us we'll say the boat struck a mine and we were the only survivors.*

Then to our surprise there followed a short burst of gunfire, as coastal batteries engaged. Crash dive! We sank thankfully to the bottom.

CHAPTER THIRTEEN

SIXTY-SIX DAYS UNDER WATER

MORALE was high. There was complete unity amongst us and our decision was duly entered in the log-book. Any suggestion of running our ship on democratic lines was ruled out. "You're still Commander," the officers told me, and the ratings, too, were convinced this was right. We certainly worked efficiently, even with so few hands aboard. The youngsters in the engine room knew their jobs and carried on without the petty officers, and, incidentally, moved into their mess, so that now we had room to stretch our legs.

As we proposed to set a course right round Britain we had to take every precaution, for the British would certainly be patrolling the approaches. They didn't mean to let any leading personality in the Reich slip away, and were well aware of the audacity of their enemy. We turned out to be right. The sea round Britain was thoroughly patrolled without relaxation for a long time after the war.

A week went by with the same tension and uncertainty all the time, but with this big difference, that we were no longer under the orders of any Command, but individuals fighting for our personal freedom. For days on end we cruised at 25 fathoms by day and at Snort depth by night in order to charge our batteries – a nerve-racking experience without a periscope. One thing we did that we had never done before – we went about dressed in escape-gear. While running on the Snort I even permitted smoking in the engine-room, as it was the only distraction left to us during these days of unremitting strain. After all, when "Snorting" the boat is well ventilated, and there is no danger from battery fumes. The Diesels themselves emit long tongues of flame when the side-valves are opened to check pressures and rates of burning. So why should we be deprived of the one pleasure still available to us?

After eighteen days without a break the crew began to get on edge, with black rings under their eyes, and faces pale and even greenish-looking from lack of daylight and fresh air. The bulkheads, too, were turning green with damp. Since we were permanently dived now we couldn't get rid of the refuse from the galley and this piled up into a revolting mess that, apart from the smell, bred flies, maggots and other vermin. Although, we were sixteen short our space was still restricted. What had been the petty-officers' mess was only 12 feet long, about 7 feet wide and exactly 6 feet 3 inches high, but twelve people had to share it. Soap ran short, but as we could only wash our clothes with salt water they couldn't dry in any case, and what we didn't wash had to be left lying about because of the lack of room in the lockers. From time to time a man on watch would come down and say he just had to get some sleep – others played card-games. And so it went on, day and night – not that it made any difference to us if it was night or day, living as we were by artificial light. We couldn't even move around the boat without permission because that might upset its trim, and our vision, naturally, was eternally limited to its bleak confines. With our bodies and minds both imprisoned, there was nothing to occupy or stimulate us, and nothing at all to enjoy – cut off as we were from nature and civilisation. However much we longed to let off steam somehow, to scream, pick a quarrel, or hit someone, we dared not break down for fear of what that might lead to – self-control is the first essential for the caged. But how long would such self-control be within our power? We were only human, and this life we were leading now seemed more than we could bear. At first the officers played cards, every now and then one of them going off to smoke a cigarette in the engine-room to ease the tension, and gradually they would go off more and more often.

Once when the Snort was down one of the Diesels stopped, and at first the engineer could not make out the reason. But we soon realised that the main couplings had been chafing and got too hot. This was honestly the last straw – here we were with neither periscope nor proper technicians, without cover of darkness and in enemy-patrolled waters; with a single engine we'd need five hours for charging. "There's no way out of it now", I thought, "we were bound to be caught in the end."

Still, our youthful crew put their backs into it magnificently, and in two days the damage was repaired. But we seemed in for a run of ill-luck, for in its turn the second Diesel stopped too, and involved us in the same repairs all over again. But come what might we had to keep cheerful, and get used to set-backs of this kind. In fact, from that time on twenty-four hours never went by without some kind of trouble cropping up. We were having to pay, now for that general overhaul we'd never had.

At times it seemed as if the enemy were after us, for whenever we raised our Snort we picked up the Radar of approaching ships or planes. While on this passage there remained only one means of guarding against surprise – to stop engines at short intervals, usually of half an hour, and to dive to "listening-depth". The object of this lay in the fact that the enemy knew about our Radar search receivers and must calculate that he couldn't now take us by surprise if he used Radar alone. For this reason, U-boat hunting groups also employed hydrophones, with which a U-boat's Diesels could be picked up at a considerable distance. If nothing was in sight on the bearing indicated by the hydrophones, the ship could be pretty certain that they had heard a U-boat. And if subsequently the U-boat was heard to stop engines, the ship could assume that the submarine was also using hydrophones, and would at once stop her own engines. We had, therefore, to carry out this manoeuvre so smartly that our surface enemy had no time by stopping engines to conceal his presence. We all expected to hear depth-charges at any moment yet how futile it would be to be drowned after the war was over! Every day things grew more critical. Often we had to use our Snort for eight days on end, as our batteries hadn't been fully charged for ages. Although the crew cared for them as if they were the most fragile porcelain sometimes one gave out and then another, and we wondered if they would last. Often we heard mines or depth-charges exploding in the distance. Perhaps they were after other U-boats?

After seven weeks of the same old faces many of us were on the verge of nervous breakdowns. With rubbish and dirt piling up everywhere there was clearly only one thing to do, namely to unload a torpedo, jam the refuse into the empty tube and fire it out by compressed air. It was then that the quarrel started that was bound to come sooner or later. The senior watch-keeper said it would save a lot of trouble to fire the torpedo instead of unloading it. In fact the best thing to do would be to fire all our torpedoes as they were no use to us, and we should have more space aboard without them. On the face of it that made sense, but realised how important It might be to be able to prove that we had not fired any torpedoes after the capitulation by showing that we still had them all aboard. To say that we had simply fired them into the sea would hardly sound convincing. After strong words had passed on both sides and the watch-keeper still refused to see reason, I bluntly ordered him to carry out my instructions. It was the first time since our company had agreed on our line of action that I had had to play the part of the disciplinarian.

As summer wore on and we moved into southern waters it grew gradually hotter. The mould was getting the upper hand, and unless we washed down the bulkheads every day they began to turn quite green. Our clothes stuck to our bodies, and as we had to wash in salt water we began to itch all over. Some of the chaps broke out into rashes, others into boils, but it couldn't be helped. We had been fifty days underwater and just had to hold out till we were off Gibraltar, when we should be able to proceed surfaced by night. How we looked forward to that! At any rate we should see the sky and the stars again, when we had almost forgotten what they looked like.

One day a man from the engine-room came to me with his hand badly swollen on the knuckle. I grew very uneasy, for in a few days his whole arm was thick and soft right up to the shoulder-blade. There was no way but to operate, although there was no doctor on board; U-boats with a Snort never carried one because they were never in action against planes. The patient just sat in the wardroom with his pale yellowish-green cheeks and the dark rings under his eyes, his long beard increasing the total ghastly effect. (It wasn't customary to shave in submarines, for this would have deprived us of protection against the cold and wet and oil).

We were cruising at 40 fathoms. Up above the sun was shining, or so we imagined. The instruments were all laid out and I brought along a bottle of Schnapps, which is the best of anaesthetics. We froze the arm and then lanced it, and an enormous quantity of matter and fluid exuded. The operation was successful. With hourly changes of bandages, in a few days the crisis passed and a great weight was taken off my mind. Under the pressure of this illness on board I had already planned to put into port and hand over the sick man to the next passenger-ship, which would have meant the end of our Argentine hopes.

But even as it was, whenever I was left alone in my cabin I began to worry. Had I done the right thing? I was responsible for the lives of thirty-one men. Even if all had freely volunteered for this enterprise, the fact remained that many were still minors. As if to confirm any doubts, I began to sense an atmosphere of discontent among the crew. The complaint came to my ears that we really should have turned back and gone home at the start, for the men who had disembarked must be home by now, whereas the remainder, who were having to put up with this miserable existence, might never see the light of day again – and I admit it did seem our underwater cruise was going to last for ever. One of the men came to me to suggest we put into a Spanish port. But we were now fully committed, and I was determined to stick fast to my resolution.

"We're going to the Argentine," I told him.

Something had to be done, for discipline was going to pieces. I would come upon a group of men muttering together, but when I approached they would suddenly fall silent. Nerves were stretched to breaking point. Day by day the same things went wrong – nothing seemed to be going smoothly. The boat was often full of vapour, which hurt our lungs and made our eyes smart, for every wave would automatically shut off the Snort valve and temporarily reduce the pressure before the valve could open and let the air rush in again – a constant change of pressure that was wearing us all out. Then as our refuse piled up we had to keep on unloading torpedoes, shooting the stuff out and then replacing the torpedo. Perhaps it would have been better to have fired off all the damned things after all and been done with it.

In the engine-room they were always bathed in oil and sweat and in general suffered worst from our abominable conditions. We hardly had any soap left. Nobody could move forward or aft without asking leave. Were we slaves or simply animals?

One day it was reported to me that one of the ratings had stolen some chocolate – a very serious offence in a U-boat. The stores are always left where everyone can see them, for there are no means of locking them away. If anybody were just to go and take anything he liked the man responsible for victualling us would never know how much was left. Here was a danger for the whole boat – and besides, you just don't steal from your own messmates. U-boat crews saw to it that that sort of thing didn't happen, and in fact it hardly ever did.

I decided to act rigorously. The crew knew my views perfectly well, and though I had never been over-strict I definitely wasn't standing for this; so without discussing the matter further I called a special muster in the fo'c'sle before supper. When my number one reported "All hands mustered for'ard", I put on my white cap, which had been lying in my locker for ages, as well as my blue uniform with all my decorations, and went to address the men. When I arrived the ship's company was brought to attention.

> "*Kameraden*, you know as well as I do why I have called you together. I don't want to preach any sermons or inflict any moralisings on you; you are all old enough to know right from wrong. Remember you have been in the finest branch of a world-famous service. In our darkest hour you bore yourselves in a way that history won't forget – they didn't call us the Sea Wolves for nothing. And are you going to let yourselves go to bits now? Go sulking around looking like whipped curs? You've lost all interest in our dash for freedom, haven't you, just because life seems too tough for you at

the moment? Because you can't see the sun and have to spend your time down in this hole and don't know what the future holds in store? How often have I heard it said, 'Oh, we should have done this or that', or, 'Our fuel won't take us to South America', or, 'We might run out of stores', or, 'Our health is being undermined'? What sort of fool do you take me for? Do you think I don't know what I'm doing or never foresaw all this? Didn't you all decide freely on this venture and put your trust in me? Well, it's too late to go back now. I demand of you that you obey my orders unquestioningly, and for my part I shall shrink from no means to do what I think right whatever the consequences. You know that I want to bring you through to freedom. Whether we shall succeed I know no more than you, but that we shall certainly fail if you go on behaving as you have been lately I do know. When it comes to stealing on board then we're on a damned slippery slope, one that leads to murder maybe, maybe to mutiny. That way we'll be just good enough to feed the rats; in fact we'll be doing the enemy's job for him. A fine end for men of the Submarine Service.

"Listen, all of you, now. When I say stealing from messmates I mean just that, because that's what happened in this boat this very morning. Nothing is more contemptible than stealing from your own messmates. The next thing we shall have to do is to put bolts on all our lockers and never trust the man in the next bunk but go slinking round like a gang of thieves looking over our shoulders for a stab in the back. But it's not coming to that because I know you to be decent men and that's why I've always trusted you. You've just let it all get too much for you. Now, for God's sake pull yourselves together and deal with anyone who lets us down as you think he should be dealt with."

I turned to walk out. The ship's company were again called to attention, and the men responded with a show of their old smartness. The thief got a severe dressing-down and for days no one would speak to him, which isn't a light punishment in a small boat where anything's better than being left alone.

A week later we threw a party to celebrate our new-found comradeship. In the last few days I had taken care to be rather aloof, but in a very short time we were all back to the spirit of our vital decision. The men had taken on a new lease of life and nobody now said that we had done the wrong thing or that we should have gone to Spain or anything of that sort. The "guilty party" himself came to me for a pardon, and became a very useful member of our small society from that time on.

But the rise in our morale could not compensate our unnatural way of life for ever. Now that we had been dived for sixty days we began to grow "mouldy', ourselves. The last patch of colour vanished from our narrow, beard-encircled faces and we no longer had any appetite but went coughing through the darkness without uttering. We did our jobs like automations and what with not seeing the light of day or having a breath of decent fresh air for two months we had in fact become so many corpses with strength neither of mind nor of body. Woodwork started to rot, condensation was perpetually dripping down the bulkheads, bunks and linen permanently damp. When they were not on watch the majority would just lie down on their bunks in a complete stupor. Often when it was too much for us we resorted to the oxygen cylinders, but by now these were almost empty. Our quarters were black with Diesel exhaust, which was inevitable, as the water pressure was becoming too great for the exhaust valves, and nearly every day great clouds of smoke rolled through the boat. The engines themselves were not exactly new, and we could never afford to rest them, so that with the constant full speed ahead the strain was beginning to tell. Now and then vital electrical parts would fail, which in all that damp was hardly surprising, but luckily the senior electrician had stayed aboard and he was an expert at his job.

At last the great day broke when I thought it safe to give the order to surface! We had come to an area where it seemed to me that we could afford to run the risk of cruising on the surface at last. Every face lit up, all thoughts were full of this, the great event. That day we had been sixty-six days under water and that night we were coming up at long last. The prospect of release from this inferno electrified us all. Everyone began to count the blessings in store for him – to feel fresh air blowing through his lungs, to look out on the sea or up to the stars in the sky. One movement only was needed for the gates of hell to fly open.

We all made ready, for by now it should by all our reckoning be dark. Every man was on his feet and wanted to go up onto the bridge. But we couldn't allow that, for Gibraltar was still too near to be healthy.

The boat rose slowly. I stood up on the hatchway ladder, and once more I laid my hand upon the hatch-securing wheel – and a very rusty wheel it had become. From the hydrophone the message came, "All clear". We rose to 10 fathoms. I gave the order for release – "Surface!" It must have rung like an enchanted formula in the ears of every man on board. Elation swept over me, a sense that life had begun again for all of us. The compressed air came hissing into our tanks, the depth-gauge in the conning-tower started moving – why, it was racing! It was like going up in a lift.

"Hatchway free!" shouted the chief engineer. "Pressure equalised!"

I raised the conning-tower hatch and climbed out onto the bridge. The senior watch-keeper came up after me and we looked about us. There was no ship anywhere in sight.

CHAPTER FOURTEEN

SOUTHERN CROSS

OVERHEAD stretched the starry vault of the sky, astern all was a-sparkle with the moon's diamond shimmer, and everywhere about us rolled a vast expanse of sea. I gazed on the universe around me with a new kind of awe. To breathe great breaths of this clear fresh air was indeed an elixir for the soul – I filled my lungs with it again and again, for after the scanty oil-laden atmosphere of our underwater prison this sea-air seemed the most precious of all gifts.

Watch was kept on the bridge. The men off-duty gathered in the control-room, but very few could see through the hatch to catch a glimpse of the stars. "Permission for one man to go on deck?"was the usual form of request aboard U-boats when somebody asked leave to go up on the bridge. The regulations prescribed that only two apart from the watch must be on deck at any time, but that wouldn't do now. Soon everybody was on deck. Only the engine-room staff had to stay below, and one wireless-operator – for we still had to watch out for the enemy's Radar; they might still be on our track, even though the last few days had passed without any disturbance at all from that quarter.

The thrill of this supreme moment gripped us all. We just stood gazing up at the stars. It was so long since we had seen them, and there were many more joys in store. We could already distinguish the stars of the southern hemisphere, and I pointed them all out to the men who had never sailed in these waters. Our culprit was up there, too, but the episode had been forgotten and we were all one again. We laughed and joked together. Oh yes, we were happy.

"Life's worth living again now!" Moses declared. "You won't get me back into that old coffin! It's worse than a dungeon!"

"All right, you're welcome to take a dinghy; it's all yours!"

The night passed swiftly, and no one felt like turning in – we were enjoying it all too much for that. It seemed a dispensation to live had been granted us. The waves ahead and the wake astern, and the porpoises all round us; I can't find words to express our joy at it all. Past hardships were forgotten it was good to be alive that night.

We had at first decided to dive at dawn, but then we put it off till sunrise, for that was a sight we didn't want to miss. The sun came up, a blood-red ball of fire above the vast stretch of water, and we all just stood and marvelled at the spectacle, every man in silence, looking and looking. As they stood there I took in properly for the first time those haggard, wrinkled faces with their sunken eyes and grey skins tinged with yellowish-green, with their blanched lips and sprawling, unkempt beards. Those faces, once fresh and healthy, had been transformed by our experience into death-masks, as if the sixty-six days of it had more than rounded off the work of the entire war. My senior watch-keeper's hair had gone quite grey.

As the daylight increased we dived leisurely back into the depths. We had decided how to divide up the twenty-four hours, in effect by transposing night and day, sleeping by day and by night surfacing and getting down to work. Watch-keeping, of course, was not affected; not that it made much difference with the light never changing, and midday and midnight indistinguishable on our twelve-hour clocks. It was at midnight, in any case, that we had our main meal, after which we went to work till daybreak, when we turned in. In that way we were fresh to enjoy the beauties of nature around us when the time came again for surfacing. During this night-cruising we still took every precaution, dismantling our AA-guns and giving them a thorough overhaul – and it was amazing to see how well they were preserved, even after all the time we had spent underwater. We reloaded them all and set a spare magazine by every gun. We also restored the watch on deck at its former strength and put the Radar search receiver into good order. If ships or planes attacked we meant to defend ourselves, for we weren't going to sell our lives for nothing. If forced to fight, we'd fight.

We had learnt in the course of our great adventure that the energy and will-power of one individual can make all the difference to the fate of everyone on board. As Commander I was bound to see that for the sake of every one of us harmony should prevail in my boat. I wore my white cap as a sign that I was responsible for carrying out our undertaking to the very end, happen what might, and I was grateful to the fate that had taught me how to handle my fellow men when I was in charge of my training-boat in the Baltic. Two years ago I would not have been up to the responsibility that now rested on my shoulders, but I was determined I was going to see that all my orders were carried out to the letter and to come down heavily on any attempt to split us into factions or to undermine discipline so long as we were at sea.

It seemed at last that the worst lay behind us and that all we had to do was to pursue our mission undiscovered in order to bring it to a successful conclusion. One disturbing thought, however, was that while we had been submerged our fuel had been reduced to 40 tons. Naturally enough, several of our men began to reckon things out and drew the inference that we could never reach Argentina, seeing how much fuel we had consumed already and how far we had still to go. It was quite true that at first sight the prospect looked pretty bleak for us. We had covered 1,800 miles since we left Christiansund, and to do that we had had to consume 40 tons of fuel, and now with only 40 tons left we had to travel another 5,500 miles. It was perfectly true that we carried tanks sufficient to store 120 tons when we set out, but in the days immediately preceding the collapse of Germany there were only 80 tons to be had. All Germany's reserves had been used up and every plan to develop synthetic substitutes or devices to make our fuel last out longer had gone to pieces. The very small extra quantity that our chief engineer had contrived to get hold of by his admirable "know how" had been exhausted very quickly.

After working things out very thoroughly and talking them over in the greatest possible detail, I came to the conclusion that we could only afford to dive in particularly critical emergencies, for diving is a very wasteful process. And on no account must we use our Snort again. So I gave orders that we were to proceed surfaced for ten hours at a time at slow speed, at about 60 revolutions on one Diesel, and that for the other fourteen hours we must rely on our electric motors. We couldn't afford to take account of any mishaps that might arise from travelling so slowly. I reckoned that we should reach our destination about the middle of August, and I hoped that by then we should still have five tons of fuel in reserve. If the fuel really did give out we planned to make a sail and cover the last stretch of the South Atlantic by making full use of the currents and winds, which were to some extent in our favour. If the worst came to the worst we could always make for Brazil.

My crew were in a much better mood. We often passed passenger ships with all their navigation lights on, for, after all, the war was over now. One night a passenger-steamer overtook us, and we caught the distant strains of dance music. People were walking up and down the promenade deck, and we looked on, itching to take action, while the giant vessel, a very mountain of light, passed unconcernedly on its way, remaining in view for a full hour. The Sea Wolf once the terror of the ocean, had become a very tame puppy indeed.

As I say, we had rigged up our Radar search gear again, and all smoking on the bridge was strictly forbidden,which may have been overdoing it, but I was taking no chances. When we proceeded surfaced by night people who wanted to smoke were allowed to do so sitting down inside the conning tower by the periscope, and also when surfaced we could tune in to the wireless, enjoy some music and, most important of all, listen to the news again. After being completely isolated from the world for two long months, we could now once more get a clearer picture of what was happening in it, and it was quite evident from the news broadcasts that things at home were very bad. We found out at last what had happened after the capitulation – obviously no development that could help us, no break-up of the victorious coalition. Germany was staggering under the full weight of defeat. Here was much food for reflection, for I was, after all, responsible for what happened to the men under my command. Once more I had to sort things out in my cabin, and I spent many unhappy hours a prey to conflicting thoughts – so far was I from being in a position to weigh up all the facts.

The crew could talk of nothing except the state of those they had left behind them, and a fearful anxiety gripped every heart. What had become of those they loved since the occupation, and particularly of the refugees who must be reduced to the most pitiful state struggling to find shelter. They would have no beds to lie on and no blankets to cover them; of their fathers and brothers there would be no news, or if there was it would be bad news, either that they were dead or crippled. And nobody could expect any help, for all would have their own problems and no time to look after anybody else. People would probably be fighting for a piece of bread, for potato-skin: old men and children would go hungry and still-births be a daily feature of existence. My own mother had stayed in Berlin all through the last battle, and I was for ever unhappily speculating what could have happened to her; and there were many others in the same plight.

The state of our boat was appaling. All the plating was rusty, and the bulkheads had gone quite green. I gave the senior watch-keeper orders to give her a thorough overhaul. She must be repainted wherever she needed it; the rust must be scraped off the ammunition, and he must see that it was properly greased. Those sixty-six days under water had told on our boat as well as of ourselves. Unfortunately the senior watch-keeper was not in sympathy with me – he insisted that the boat was bound to be sunk off the Argentine coast anyhow and that an overhaul was sheer waste of time and energy. I told him to carry out my orders and not to argue. In this the ratings were with me to a man and the state of the boat improved considerably. The big magazines for the 2-centimetre quick-firing guns were taken to pieces, thoroughly cleaned and put back. When one seaman left cartridges carelessly lying around on the deck so as to make his work lighter I pointed out the danger of explosion and told him to carry out his duties precisely as he had been taught to do at the gunnery-school. The senior watch-keeper thought that he knew better, however, and made some disparaging remarks for me to overhear. I sent for him in my cabin and gave him a dressing-down, but he openly took his stand against me, arguing that I had no right to give him orders and was no longer his superior by any authority whatever.

This was the very limit. No one was prevented from expressing anxieties or even criticisms to me in decent terms, but this was different, and I decided not to argue the point.

I was bitterly aware that his aggressive attitude threatened us with a split among the crew. I had no official authority behind me and my superiors to back me up, so I had to handle the matter alone. As a matter of fact it was this officer's fault that our periscope had been carried away, which might have been fatal to us when we "snorted". He had forgotten to house the periscope during a crash dive and the result was that the wires had snapped under the water pressure at 60 fathoms and the thing had fallen with a crash into the boat, smashing all the prisms.

I decided that his present behaviour, added to the mishaps for which he was responsible, justified my taking extreme measures. I accordingly relieved the senior watch-keeper of all his duties in front of the whole ship's company, and forbade anybody to carry out his orders or to discuss anything concerning our voyage with him. The junior watch-keeper took over in his place.

By this time we were approaching the Cape Verde Islands, and we expected their rocky peaks to come into sight at any moment – it was so long since we had sighted land that our eyes were trying to pierce the dark like gimlets. As dawn began to break first one shadow loomed ahead and then another. We didn't bother to dive, for there would certainly be no look-out on the islands.

When the sun rose the massive cliffs rising sheer out of the sea were an impressive spectacle. We began to make out fields and green meadows on the slopes, and fishing boats gay with coloured sails. To be on the safe side we kept at night-periscope depth – true, our remaining periscope was short, but no one in these parts was going to look out for the disturbance that propellers cause when turning close under the surface. Soon we passed an island that could not have been more than a thousand metres away at most. Everybody got a chance to look through the periscope, and, delighted with the actual sight of men working in the open air, we all felt we really must spend some days here to recuperate – surely the Allies wouldn't be hunting U-boats in the Cape Verde Islands...

I saw in my "pilot" that some of the islands of the group were uninhabited, and the crew jumped at the idea of landing on one of them. We made for Branca Island and surfaced off it, feeling by now quite secure. Everybody came up on deck to admire the dead-calm sea with the rocks mirrored on its stretches of blue, and the white beaches beyond. Dolphins sported all around us, seeming as if they were trying to leap up onto our bows; we were grateful to them for their carefree play. Of human life we saw no sign through our binoculars, except a few fishermen's huts which were probably only shelters used during rough weather. At this time of year everybody would be on the larger islands. Carefully we approached the shore as close as we could, using our electric motors, the water so clear that we could see every rock and shoal: but here the breakers were so fierce that we decided to anchor. Later on we meant to make for shore by dinghy.

The Cape Verde Islands lie in shark-infested waters, but our first hesitation about bathing was soon over come, because the presence of so many dolphins showed there was no danger, and the water in any case was so clear that we would have had plenty of time to see a man-eating shark approach. Actually it is not generally known that dolphins, which are much faster and more agile and always move in large "schools", can drive off or even kill a shark many times their size. There have even been instances of dolphins saving men from sharks by forming a protective ring round the swimmer and pushing him to the land by the weight of their bodies. Our efforts to go ashore in dinghies were upset by the breakers, so we had to content ourselves with the view and the joy of being still alive and in such a beautiful place as this. We had great fun paddling the little yellow dinghies around, and now and then one or other of the men would try to race a dolphin or even to dive on to its head, but they never came anywhere near it, in fact I don't think the dolphins ever worried about us, they were far too nimble. The night was clear and warm and we had a celebration on board to wipe out all memories of the quarrels we had had in the nerve-wracking days of our underwater voyage. For the first time since I don't know how long, we all sang together and were a happy boat again and when we thought of our fellow-countrymen dragging out their weary existence behind barbed wire it was vividly brought home to us that nothing is more precious than freedom.

After we had all had our morning dip we weighed anchor and our single Diesel engine began its monotonous drone again. Steering a southward course we got a fix from the last island in the Cape Verde group and soon left it far astern. All round us the sea spread calm and unruffled and the sun shone high in the heavens. All the men were lying around on deck, and their pallid bodies had begun to turn brown. It was certainly good for them. Rashes and swellings vanished in a few days, and haggard fretful faces began to fill out again. There was no more snapping and quarrelling, and people who would not speak to each other before became friends again and joked and laughed together. We kept a hose on deck and used it constantly to keep ourselves cool in the great heat, but naturally everybody wanted to bathe in the sea.

The ideal thing would be surf-riding behind the boat, and, as we had plenty of wood and, of course, rope, in a day we had our surf-board ready. But it wouldn't do to be dragged astern; we had to arrange to surf-ride in such a way that there'd be less danger of being caught up in the screws. So the line was made fast to our bows and then the more enterprising amongst us clambered on to the swaying board. Another rope was tied to it to make it fast, and then the surf-rider could ride it standing or kneeling or lying flat: he'd go spinning along fine over the ripples, gently lifted and dropped by the swell. It was magnificent sport. As a precaution we tied a strong belt round the rider and several men hung on to the rope. If he fell into the sea it was their job to haul him on board so he should keep clear of the screws and we need not stop our engine. That way, too, we saved ourselves manoeuvring to pick him up, which would have wasted time and fuel, not to speak of the danger from sharks.

As soon as day broke the first man would be on the board while the others queued up. Of course we all swallowed a lot of salt water, for we were none of us experts at it and most of us had only seen surf-riding on newsreels. Yet even when the weather took a turn for the worse, my crew were not to be deterred from their favourite pastime. Admittedly, quite a number badly grazed their legs against the barnacles on the boat's side when they clambered onto or off the surf-board. But that didn't put them off. No one caught cold – on the contrary, they had all taken on a new lease of life. Scarcely anyone slept below, for the air was too foetid and clammy, besides being very hot, so the men used hammocks spread on blankets or cushions up on deck. We had all our meals on deck, too. I'm glad no one saw us. Just imagine a warship with hammocks and sun blinds slung between the guns! We used to have target practice with empty bottles; or else fish either with harpoons or handgrenades to vary our rations – flying fish make very good eating. We specially admired the little jelly-fish with their iridescent membranes gliding idly with the wind. In submarines you have a great advantage over other ships because you are brought into touch with the astonishing deep-sea world. Most men who put to sea nowadays know nothing of the opportunities that lie within their reach. But we in submarines had long learnt to ponder over the infinite riches of the underwater world and the living things that dwell in it. Never till now, however, had we been so impressed with the endless variety of all that immense colourfulness teeming below the surface.

Whenever a ship passed by we used to make a detour so as to keep well out of sight. But then we began to wonder whether all the fuss was really necessary when it would be so much easier to camouflage our boat. So we set to cutting linen and sailcloth into strips and spread them out till from a distance we must have looked exactly like a harmless cargoboat. Everybody had an inspiration. We even rigged up a funnel by cutting up a sheet of tin and planting it carefully on top of an open case with an oily rag inside it, and connecting that to a compressed-air tube to help it burn more brightly. Whenever the need arose great clouds of smoke puffed skyward, scattering sparks as they belched from our "funnel", and the effect was so convincing that we never had to dodge a ship again.

One day a man on the surf-board gave a terrifying yell, for an enormous fish was swimming alongside. We wondered if it was a shark. I had never seen such an enormous sea monster in all my life, but luckily it turned out to be a whale. If the man was terrified the whale was quite unimpressed. It just swam three times round the boat and then followed alongside for several hours, while we threw sardines to it. For a time it became our mascot and our Moses suggested it might give us a helpful tow if it felt inclined.

Now we were approaching the equator, and the sun was blazing down from a cloudless sky without a breath of wind to ruffle the sea. We were in the doldrums, the calm waters that the old sailing ships used to dread, and to protect our heads and necks from the burning sun we all devised special types of headgear. My own sun helmet was a yard across. Next day we were due to cross the line, and so we organised our ritual on the same scale as we had done en-route for Freetown, except that this time we went through it up on deck. I played Neptune. The Chief of Police beat the wretched victims with his broad sword, giving one or two a particularly hearty crack. But just as the celebration was at its height we picked up the sound of an aeroplane and hurriedly rigged up our FuMB apparatus. Were they going to find us at last? The look-outs gave up watching the ducking of our initiates to turn their attention in other directions. Though we could still see nothing the hum of engines was incessant. Should we dive or shouldn't we? At any rate we manned the guns and loaded them. Thetis took her station by a 3.7-centimetre gun while the Physician-in-ordinary and the barber snatched up machine-guns. The whole court took up their stations in case we had to dive. It may have looked funny, but it was very serious for us, the last of the U-boat crews that had so lately been the terror of the high seas, all rigged up in fancy dress and determined to fight for our lives. But it never came to that. The drone of the plane's engines, probably only a passenger transport, gradually died away, so we were able to finish our ritual, if with rather mixed feelings.

Once our ex-senior watch-keeper lost his automatic, which was very serious indeed. When it comes to stealing firearms things have reached a pretty pass. We suspected one of the wireless operators who was rather unpopular with us because of his aversion to any sort of extra work. All the men's quarters were turned upside down, and a thorough search began which, however, yielded no results. I talked over the affair with the men in whom I had the greatest confidence and told them that it was imperative for them to discover the culprit. We said nothing more about it for the time being, but after four days I received a report that the automatic had been found in a transmitter, and that the wireless operator was the thief. I summoned him to my cabin and he made a full confession. Then I called the men together in the fo'c'sle and we administered another dressing down. His head was shaven, he was forbidden to go on deck for a fortnight and was kept under arrest aft by the torpedo-tube, where he had to survive on bread and water. Naturally no one spoke to him, for a man who steals firearms is beyond the pale, and we kept a close watch over him till the end of our cruise.

So, the days slipping by, we still pursued our unending course, and not for a moment did the gurgle of our wake and bow-wave cease. We were all as brown as berries and would sit dangling our legs in the water when we weren't eating or drinking. There was very little work to do. As for laundry, that problem was solved by hanging it on a line towed astern of the boat for an hour, for we had discovered that for the best laundry you can't beat deep seawater and a turbulent wake. Our quarters glittered like new, the rust was scraped away and the tropical sun had dried out all the woodwork.

One day we learnt from the wireless that U-530 had put into the River Plate. We listened anxiously. What was going to become of the ship's company? Would they be handed over or be allowed to remain in Argentina, the country of which we had such high hopes? Unfortunately we knew no Spanish and it would have been much more to the point if we could only have picked up the news at its source instead of having to depend on censored transmissions from other countries.

Time passed quickly. At one time we saw the haze of light in the sky that betokened Rio de Janeiro. We were proceeding now more and more to the south, and it was colder again – we had left the tropics behind us. As we had been detailed for operations in the north Atlantic we had no charts of the southern hemisphere, so we laid our course by dead reckoning and made charts for ourselves. Fortunately we had books aboard that told us the longitude and latitude of all the most important coast towns, and we took care to steer clear of the coast of Brazil, which we knew was very dangerous with its rocks and reefs. It wasn't worth running any risks to cut a few hours off our voyage.

Then we heard that U-530 had been handed over to the United States with all its complement as prisoners of war. This depressing news was a heavy blow to all our hopes of freedom, and in the light of it I had to reconsider everything afresh. Brought up sharp against reality, I could no longer indulge any illusions. What were we to do now? Perhaps the best thing might he to put into Brazil or Uruguay, or should we just sink our boat off the Argentine coast and chance our luck? It wasn't a bad idea, and now that our countrymen had been handed over to the enemy it certainly seemed the best way to escape a prisoner-of-war cage. On this assumption the majority did in fact get ready to abandon ship, sewing knapsacks and gathering their essentials together. Some went so far as to pack up their tools, hoping to find jobs as fitters ashore. Others, fed on adventure stories and Wild West films, worked themselves into a state of great excitement, conjuring up an extremely odd picture of South America – which, by the way, might well account for the motives of the man who stole the automatic pistol.

So far I had always taken the men into my confidence. I never wanted to use my position as Commander to impose a dictatorship and lose my crew's faith, so I took no part in the arguments for or against, especially since, to tell the truth, I hadn't made up my mind myself. I had to make a grave decision, and one that took some thinking over, for I knew that a false step now would endanger the future of everyone aboard – you can't take enemy War Crimes Tribunals lightly. There was an overwhelming majority in favour of scuttling the boat and trying our luck, a project that in a way sounded attractive enough. My newly appointed senior watch-keeper was the oldest man on board, and to my mind the best fitted to discuss these important matters with me. Every day we talked things over, and at night I went on watch with him – we must decide something, for the men wanted to know just where they stood. I played for time. On no account must we split into rival factions, but there were only a few days left and we had to come to some conclusion. My talks with the senior watch-keeper had clarified my mind and I began to see that the consequences of sinking our ship could be very serious, in fact that they were bound to be serious. So I concluded that we must not consider any such course of action, and my decision was unshakable.

There could be no question of Buenos Aires as we had no charts, and even if we had any it would be far too dangerous to risk the shallows of a river passage, 100 miles up to the Argentine capital, without a pilot. I decided, therefore, to put in to Mar del Plata, whose lighthouse should be in sight in two days by our reckoning. It was at this point that I fell-in the ship's company, knowing that if I was to carry through what had to be done and what, if I knew anything about it, was going to be done, I must make myself quite clear. Everybody hung on my words, for they knew very well that the ultimate decision must have been taken by now; but many still hoped we would sink the boat and had their things all ready packed for going ashore. I began;

> "Men of the submarine service, I'm proud of you. We have done something that no one is likely to do again. It's now three and a half months since we decided on our great project, and now we've carried it out. We all know it hasn't been easy. Early on we lost all our specialist petty officers except two, specialists who for a complicated mechanism like our boat seemed indispensable, especially in view of the long voyage that lay before us and the fact that we had to do without the usual refit; yet in spite of everything, we did it. Our engines are in perfect working order, everything aboard, except the periscope, in good condition. The engine-room personnel most particularly deserve our gratitude. Without exception they've carried out their duties to the full, both under the burning tropic sun and when we were dived. The rest of you – as is plain

to see – have cleaned out and painted up this boat of ours till it's become just what it ought to be, a model submarine. I know only too well the work you have put into it. If only we were homeward bound now how proud and pleased we should all be! Well, the voyage is over now. When I look at your bronzed and healthy faces I can feel content. You've shown your mettle, shown that you can be trusted through thick and thin.

"But now we must make our final decision, for I don't want to do anything without consulting you. We have the alternative of either sinking our boat and landing to face who knows what – or else of putting in to Mar del Plata. And I want to put both sides to you as they appear to me.

"There's no difficulty about scuttling the boat. But what happens then? Immediately after we've paddled ashore in our dinghies we come to the critical question that none of us can solve. We must destroy them or we shall be traced the moment we land. But dinghies don't burn quickly or easily, being made of rubber, and, what's more, the flames can be seen a long way off. Besides, would we have time to bury them? Well, anyway, let's assume that all goes well. We say goodbye and set off in thirty-two different directions, for it would hardly be advisable to march off together. Personally, I wouldn't be so badly off as I have friends in the capital and am in a more fortunate position than yourselves. But now let's think of you. You would have to make your way wearing German uniforms, not knowing the language and with no money in your pockets. I, myself, have the advantage of knowing English and French, but some time or other one of you is bound to be discovered by the police, and then the whole area will be cordoned off and thoroughly combed. The Allies will offer a reward for us, the papers and the wireless will broadcast the story. Could you hope under such conditions to conceal yourselves indefinitely! If any of you were to try, his name and particulars would be posted at every police station, and you can't lead a normal life or start afresh under an alias. Once discovered, who knows what we would be suspected of? One thing is certain, however, that we should all be held responsible for sinking our boat after the war was over, with malice aforethought as their propaganda would say. Just think what charges might be brought against you if U-977 were sunk, and what the consequences could be. It would be a bitter ending for our great adventure, for once caught we could certainly not hope to be set free in the foreseeable future. Supposing, on the other hand, we enter harbour, then nothing can possibly happen to us. We start with a clean sheet. If our luck's out and we do get handed over, at any rate we shall be able to look back on the fact that we have lived as free men for three months longer than our fellow countrymen at home. Which of you would have missed this voyage, for all its hardships? For most of you it will be the greatest experience of your lives. The time hasn't been wasted, for we should certainly have spent these months as prisoners of war under very different circumstances.

"In my opinion, there's only one course open to us. We must put into an Argentine port. Think it all over carefully, but don't imagine I want to bring any sort of pressure to bear on you. If you reject my solution, then, seeing that obviously I can do nothing against thirty-one men, this is what you must do: one of you, backed by the majority of the crew, must place me under restrain, and from that moment take over full responsibility as Commander of this boat, answering for all of you.

"In an hour I shall expect the senior watch-keeper to report to me with your decision."

When I had finished the majority of the crew came down on my side without much ado. I gave special orders that nothing whatsoever on board was to be damaged and no equipment destroyed.

The 17th of August 1945 was a brilliantly sunny day. We first made out the Argentine coastline, and then the lighthouse; when this last came into view the whole crew fell in on deck. There was no one missing, as we were still too far from the shore for anyone to have the chance to slip away secretly in the night. We had to be on our guard, because several men, under the impression we were going to enter harbour during the hours of darkness, had got it into their heads that they could make a getaway, which would have wrecked our entire plan, as it would then have been hard to prove that fugitives had not landed together with members of our crew. Meanwhile, my senior watch-keeper, on watch for the last time, stood by me keeping an eye on the revolution indicator to make sure that the engines maintained their correct speed.

An albatross came along with us. He first flew over the boat, and then settled down on the water and let us pass him, perhaps four feet away. He looked at the conning-tower with his tiny eyes as if to say "You do look odd with all those beards, Where on earth do you come from?" We opened a tin of sardines, and every time the bird flew back over the boat we threw him a fish. He must have been enjoying himself, because he kept it up a long time. It was only when we tried to give him breadcrumbs that he flew away.

While we were still outside the three-mile limit we flashed in English the signal *German submarine*, and stopped our engines. Several fishing-smacks came out to look at us with great curiosity and seemed to be very much impressed by our long beards. Very soon the Argentine minesweeper PY 10 and two submarines came alongside and informed us in English that an advance party would be coming out. Not long afterwards the latter, composed of one officer with several petty officers and ratings, appeared aboard a motor-launch and took over without further delay. With their immaculate white uniforms they made a favourable impression, and their bearing left nothing to be desired. I received the Argentine officer on deck and conducted him to the conning-tower, while his subordinates dispersed themselves about the boat. He told me his orders were to bring us into harbour and that it was his duty to prevent our scuttling the boat or damaging her in any way. I explained to him that I had no intention of doing anything of the kind I also suggested that I should be responsible for taking the boat into harbour, as my crew could only understand German and it was very difficult for anybody unfamiliar with our complex machinery to handle her properly. He accepted my word of honour and so it was that I gave my last orders as Commander of U-977.

CHAPTER FIFTEEN

"You Hid Hitler"

THE GREY morning light was streaming through the scuttle of my cabin aboard the cruiser *Belgrano* when the bugle sounding the "Relieve-decks" roused me from my reveries and brought me face to face with reality. I wasn't a boy sailing across the lakes of Brandenburg any longer, nor an over-confident young enthusiast reporting for service with the Sea Wolves. Nor was I Commander of U-977 any more. No, I was just a prisoner of war in the hands of the Argentine Navy; on board an old cruiser, locked in an officer's cabin. Outside sentries were posted to watch my movements, and somewhere on board my companions must be waiting in their cabins like mine, all keyed up with suspense for this momentous day. I fell to wondering whether they had slept well and woken refreshed, or whether, like me, they had lain awake thinking about our great experience and wondering what the immediate future held in store. My crew, too, who had carried the job through to the end and stoically borne the frightful nervous strain of those sixty-six days underwater so bravely and so well, where were they now? What was to become of them?

A rating, a short fellow with black hair and in a white uniform, came in, bringing me an excellent breakfast. He gaped at me, agog with curiosity, as if I was some strange creature in a zoo; it must have been my impressive beard and maybe, too, he had read and heard all kinds of stories about the secret German "submarinos". A small pot of delicious coffee, real coffee which smelt quite wonderful, soon dispelled my weariness. It was just as well, for the moment had come when I needed all my strength of mind and body. Just then there was a knock on my cabin door and two officers entered; they had come to fetch me for further interrogation by the naval officer in charge of the base. As one of them spoke English I inquired about my men, and he told me that they were all right and being well looked after.

Up in the wardroom I was again received politely, and we proceeded at once to the interrogation, which turned on three main issues. First, the sinking of the Brazilian steamer *Bahia*; secondly, my arrival so long after Germany had capitulated, and, thirdly, whether I had at any time carried anybody of political importance on board U-977. There were also a number of subsidiary questions, but as I could answer them all with clarity and conviction and referred repeatedly to my ship's papers, the sceptical look in the faces of my questioners began to disappear. The naval officer in charge informed me that all the papers I had given to him when I handed over my boat the day before were now in process of translation for checking by experts. As soon as these were received back it would be much simpler to clear the whole matter up.

U-530, which had put in before us and before the *Bahia* was sunk, had produced no papers at all. But U-530 had arrived before the death of Hitler and so was beyond suspicion. I pointed out that the fact that we had put in with our full outfit of torpedoes and that all our navigational data was available should absolve us, too, from suspicion. Every man aboard U-977 was fully aware that aggressive action after the Allied victory would have served no purpose whatever and would certainly have entailed most serious consequences. The Flotilla Commander went on to ask why exactly we should pick on Argentina for our surrender. That question wasn't hard to answer. The rules of war provide that all war material belonging to a defeated power shall become the property of the victors, and so the Soviet Union must now be in possession of all our improvements in technique. I had therefore taken care to carry out Admiral Dönitz's order to surrender – as soon as I had verified it – in such a way as to ensure that it should be advantageous to a nation which had already displayed such chivalry towards the German Navy in the matter of the pocket battleship *Graf Spee*. I had also to consider the welfare of my crew. There was no other enemy country from which they could expect such good treatment. There had never been any hatred between Germany and Argentina, only a condition of honourable belligerency, and that for a relatively short time only.

"But I must admit, *Herr Kapitän*," I added, "that other factors weighed with me as well. I did hope that during the sixty-six days when we were heading underwater for these hospitable shores there might be some revolutionary change in the sphere of international politics. But I fear my hopes were vain."

It was obvious that what I said impressed him, though he did not reply.

It would be superfluous to give a detailed account of all that happened in the days and weeks that followed. The Argentine authorities were persuaded my account was correct. But unfortunately, while the inquiry was still proceeding, a Montevideo paper called *El Dia* began to run a story that Hitler had fled on board my boat to Patagonia and thence on to the Antarctic. It was easy to see what effect this was bound to have all over the world just after a full search had failed to disclose any trace of the head of the Third Reich under the ruins of the Chancellery in Berlin. Everywhere people fell for the scare started in Montevideo. Newspapers all over the world came out with the most sensational stories and all the time there was I, a prisoner, forced to sit by in silence. I really didn't know which infuriated me most, the irresponsible sensation-mongers or the reports that reached me about the unchivalrous, shortsighted way in which the once proud armed forces of Germany were being dispersed by the victors.

Then one day I had a great surprise. I was brought before an Anglo-American Commission, composed of high-ranking officers especially despatched to Argentina to investigate the mysterious case of U-977. These gentlemen were very obstinate indeed.

"You have stowed Hitler away," they told me. "Come on, where is he?"

When I could tell them no more than I had already told the Argentinians they got very impatient indeed, and no wonder, for the voyage of U-977 was still hitting the headlines. Not one paper acknowledged the skill and endurance that had gone to make this first long underwater journey under such conditions. No, every news story, every report, feature article and leader turned on the same stale old theme of Heinz Schaeffer, who had stowed Hitler away. So, with Heinz Schaeffer actually standing before them in the flesh, it was only natural these gentlemen should be on their mettle to extract information about the Führer, whom they were so anxious to capture alive in spite of his being for so long reported dead.

To put me under still greater pressure they asked for me to be handed over to the United States, and before long I landed up in a camp for important prisoners-of-war at Washington, where I found a number of high-ranking German officers. My crew and my boat followed. For weeks on end, day after day, the Americans repeated the charge: "You stowed Hitler away." for weeks on end I tried to make them see how nonsensical the whole thing was – actually I could no more prove that I hadn't than they could show that I had, which simply brought us to a deadlock. The *Bahia* charge was different, however, and this they pressed more and more warmly. All our navigational data, even the presence of every one of our ten torpedoes didn't convince them – we might have carried fourteen torpedoes for all they knew, some U-boats did at times. Besides, how were they to know that we hadn't made false entries in our log-book?

But at last something happened that cleared us completely. The Brazilian Ministry of Marine issued full details of the weather conditions at the time and place where the *Bahia* went down. These were compared with the meteorological observations taken the same day aboard U-977, and of course they didn't tally, as we were in a completely different area at the time. Nobody went quite so far as to suggest that we had faked our meteorological reports, and so the charge was dropped.

Just before that happened I experienced a typical example of "screening". Otto Wehrmut, Commander of U-530, was suddenly brought face to face with me, after which we were left in the same room together. We had never met before, but we saw at once what all this added up to. They were hoping that in the first flush of our joyful reunion we would so far forget ourselves as to discuss, in front of all their dictaphones, the whole inside story of the ghost convoy. They must have been very annoyed when nothing emerged from our talk save the true facts about the completely independent voyages of both our submarines.

When I had spent many months in captivity an English friend sent me a cutting from an English newspaper which reproduced a photograph that really did shatter me. It showed an explosion at sea. Of course I had seen many explosions at sea during the war, when the Sea Wolves showed their teeth. I knew how these explosions used to disturb the leaders of the United Nations back in the days when the German radio put out one special transmission after another to tell the world of the impressive successes our U-boats were scoring. But the photograph in the newspaper cutting that lay in front of me that morning bore the headline The end of U-977. It was clear from the text that my fine boat had been sunk, on the surface, by torpedo fire by order of the US War Department. I comforted myself with the thought that, just as it had saved all our lives and brought us safely across the Atlantic, so equally well it might have made a steel coffin for us down at the bottom of the sea. We had intended to present our boat to the Argentine Navy, but we overlooked the complexity of inter-continental agreements.

It was obvious that everything about our U-boat had proved of the utmost interest to the Allies. Indeed, their experts soon appreciated what our improvements in technique could have meant. For instance, Dr Vannevar Bush, the leading specialist in the United States on the potentialities of modern weapons, has said that had our latest class of U-boat been produced in time they would have so steadied the swing of the pendulum that the whole course of the war would have been different, and the outcome very doubtful.

When the Russians occupied East Germany they took over most of the U-boats under construction in the yards at Danzig, Stettin and Königsberg, and it may also be taken for granted that they have now got the Walther engine for super U-boats, whereas the Western Powers only got hold of a few spare parts which were later taken to London. I shall make no comment on the new situation created by the construction of a large Soviet submarine fleet based on German techniques, some say as many as a thousand boats, beyond mentioning Dr Bush's warning that should the West find themselves at war with an enemy in a position to make use of the most up-to-date methods of naval warfare, they would have to start all over again from the beginning to discover a way to deal with the U-boat menace, and to make that start from a position highly unfavourable to themselves.

The real paradox lies in the fact that it is thanks to Radar that the submarine has once again become the formidable threat that it constitutes today. So far it has remained the only weapon immune from all methods of detection. Aircraft, rockets and V-weapons can be located and plotted, thus making it possible to take counter-action. But the latest type of submarine can cruise submerged across whole oceans and will possibly be in a position to fire atomic weapons into enemy ports and production centres. Experience to date seems to show that the possibility of development of long-range Asdic underwater detectors is doubtful. Variations of salinity, currents and temperature differences will always cause considerable inaccuracies by interference with the transmitted and reflected electro-acoustic waves.

Perhaps the best way of defeating large submarines is by small ones equipped with acoustic torpedoes similar to our own *Zaunkönig* type. But will it succeed? The submarine menace probably means the end of large capital ships, which have ceased to repay their cost of construction (ships like the *Bismarck* or the *Missouri* cost as much to build as a town of a hundred thousand inhabitants), and which the potentialities of modern submarines would appear to have rendered obsolete.

But for those discoveries which will now benefit other sea powers

Germany paid a heavy price. The casualties in our submarine service were catastrophic. Vice-Admiral Assman writes in the American review *Foreign Affairs*, that out of 40,000 men who served in our U-boats 30,000 lost their lives. We had some 720 U-boats at sea and 640 of them were sunk, and yet whether those figures would deter another power from trying to secure command of the seas by the use of super submarines is highly doubtful.

In Washington I was treated decently in every way, although things were rather different at other places where the US Supreme Command was less able to make its presence felt. When I was cleared at last they shipped me back to Germany, my crew having already been repatriated. The voyage was uneventful, but all the German harbours were congested with Allied ships, so we were landed at Antwerp, where for "technical reasons" I became a prisoner of the British instead of the Americans. They immediately proceeded to start up the whole business about stowing Hitler away all over again. I was subjected to more interrogations, and the British behaved as though their American cousins hadn't done their job thoroughly enough. Of course I had nothing new to say but they were obviously under the spell of the legend of U-977; so much so, in fact, that instead of putting me in an ordinary prisoner-of-war camp they installed me in a place of detention for very serious cases, where I was treated as if I had been some prominent leader of the Third Reich.

But, being able to explain *everything* to their eventual satisfaction, I still managed to survive and so finally found myself a civilian again and a free man – if you can talk of freedom in an occupied country.

I now began to have to steer a different sort of course through post-war Germany's sea of ruins, poverty and general distress, which was in its way just as great an ordeal as steering a course across the Atlantic to Argentina. And at that stage, as I have explained already, I came up against the same old story in the streets of Düsseldorf. Apparently the author of this book, which had then just come out in Buenos Aires, was much cleverer than all the intelligence officers of all the Allied services put together. *Señor* Ladislas Szabo's opening remarks struck me as quite farcical, the more so because the news reports only gave disjointed quotations in a highly sensational style. For all that I wanted to read the book, and some time later a friend in the Argentine did send me over a copy of this very book *Hitler is Alive*.

I opened it with great excitement and was quite staggered by the sub-title, which was typical of the whole thing:

The new *Berchtesgaden in Antarctica*.

Then came a dedication to the English poet G K Chesterton, of all people. There followed a preface by one Clemente Cimorra, who declared that Szabo's arguments were highly impressive and it would be a fair deduction to make from them that the bird of ill omen, Hitler, had now spread his wings over "fourteen million square kilometres of Antarctic snow". Next came an open letter to George C Marshall, Molotov, Ernest Bevin and Georges Bidault informing them that on the 16th July 1945 the Buenos Aires paper *Critica* had published a thoroughly detailed account of Hitler's flight and precise details of his hiding-place. Since then the story had been borne out in every detail. And finally Szabo called upon the four powers to pursue the German dictator to his lair and lay their hands on him at once lest there should be a revival of Nazism in Germany.

As this open letter was written in March 1947 it must have been drafted long after the interrogation of Otto Wehrmut and myself was over. Yet Szabo's first chapter is called *El Enigma de los Submarinos* ('the mystery of the submarines') and in fact deals with the surrender of U-530 at Mar del Plata. He goes on to draw conclusions which would I imagine turn Edgar Wallace green with envy in his grave.

The next chapter concerns my own ship, U-977, and naturally interested me particularly. Unfortunately it loses its effect because the writer obviously knows as much about a U-boat as an Eskimo about Central Africa. A few extracts will show what I mean. For instance, he cites it as a highly suspicious fact that both submarines were amply provided with cigarettes, whereas normally smoking was strictly forbidden on U-boats. Well, anyone who reads this book will appreciate that in fact it was not normally forbidden except when dived. As both U-boats had cruised a considerable distance underwater, however, far longer than anybody anticipated, they naturally entered harbour with a large store of cigarettes still intact. So our Sherlock Holmes was off on completely the wrong scent.

Again, on the numbers of the crew, Szabo writes that U-boats of the U-977 class carried a normal complement of sixteen to eighteen at most. "So it was all the more suspicious that we had arrived in Argentina with thirty-two on board."

The rest of it is on the same level. On page 109 he writes that we were forbidden to use our wireless, so as not to give away our position, and yet on page 111 he blithely remarks that we learned through the wireless that Wehrmut had put in to Mar del Plata. But while you would gather from the first part of the work that either Wehrmut or I had carried Hitler aboard our own boat, the second suddenly takes on quite a different note: apparently there was a sort of phantom convoy which we were supposed to be escorting, although in fact we ourselves were quite unaware of the task we were carrying out. Jules Verne would have been delighted with this conception.

The book, as a whole, is lavishly illustrated with pictures of Hitler and Eva Braun and a girl in charge of two boys who "looked very like Hitler". There are pictures of our submarines and of men in Arctic dress and the ruins of the Chancellery in Berlin, with American Commandos searching in the Führer's air-raid shelter. There are quotations from speeches by Edda Ciano, and various other newspaper reports all cunningly mixed up which piece together an amazing thesis about our voyage. There are also references to the expedition to Antarctica of the German aircraft carrier *Schwabenland* in 1938. And here the author reaches his climax: "In 1938 the *Schwabenland*, by order of Admiral Dönitz, had set up the new Berchtesgaden... somewhere in Antarctica..." Thither, in 1945, Hitler, with his wife and children, had betaken himself, but U-530 and U-977, their convoy duties done, had preferred to turn back northwards to Argentina.

Despite the above remarkable information a woman reporter on a Buenos Aires newspaper actually went one better and claimed to have interviewed Hitler somewhere in Patagonia, but I'm afraid the only impact that it had on me was to make me laugh.

What was more serious was my discovery that in Germany itself there was widespread a sort of mystical premonition that one day Hitler would return. People just refused to believe that the Führer was really dead and secretly looked to the day when he would come back from some unknown Elba. The really serious side of the sensational stories that emanated from Montevideo and Buenos Aires was the possibility that their authors might unintentionally create a very dangerous myth which could serve as a pretext for Germans to sit back and wait. I can conceive of nothing more harmful for the future of Germany and indeed of Europe than nebulous wishful thinking of that kind. God helps those who help themselves and not those who are forever waiting for ghosts to return from the grave to do their work for them.

It is mainly this which has impelled me to publish the truth about the journey of my boat, U-977, but there is also another reason. Only a few months ago I read in the world's press that the US submarine *Pickerell*, fitted with a German-type Snorchel, had carried out an "absolutely record" passage of twenty-one days under water. If one must speak of "records" in this connection, let not the performance of U-977 be forgotten, to whose crew belongs the honour of having accomplished one of the first long-range underwater passages in the history of the sea.

As for myself, I decided from the day I first met the Argentinians that the best thing would be to make my home in Argentina and so escape from a world that had lost all sense of decency. For there is nothing the defeated appreciate more than that their victors should have a decent respect for them.

So I am living in Argentina today. Under its flag I have found the peace and quiet that I required to write this book. Beneath the southern stars my memories of the German U-boat service, of all our hard-fought battles and of the sixty-six days that U-977 cruised underwater have come to life again. And to Argentina I have taken with me the greatest thing the Second World War left me – a faith unshaken in the German people.